Tulipan Doily,
page 40

30+ Fun Weekend Projects!™

Barista Cowl,
page 46

With Love Coaster,
page 42

Table of Contents

Mosaic Shawl,
page 59

Rock Ridge Shawl,
page 22

Stripes Microwave Bowl Cozy, *page 12*

Rooster Table Runner

Design by Lisa McDonald

Skill Level

 ■■■□ INTERMEDIATE

Finished Measurements

10¼ inches wide x 54 inches long

Materials

- Scheepjes Softfun light (DK) weight cotton/acrylic yarn (1¾ oz/153 yds/50g per ball):
    5 balls #2530 cloud
    1 ball each #2412 snow, #2510 dove, #2601 graphite, #2492 Bordeaux and #2621 mustard
- Size F/5/3.75mm crochet hook or size needed to obtain gauge
- Stitch markers: 4
- Tapestry needle

Gauge

22 sc = 4 inches; 22 rows = 4 inches

Pattern Notes

Join with slip stitch as indicated unless otherwise stated.

Each square on the Chart depicts 1 single crochet stitch.

Read the Chart as follows:

Odd-numbered rows: Read and change colors from right to left.

Even-numbered rows: Read and change colors from left to right.

For easier stitching, work Chart with small skeins (or bobbins) of each color. Do not cut or finish off colors until work with each color is complete.

Carry color not in use on wrong side to bring it across and/or up to the next stitch where it will be used. When you are crocheting the right-side rows, the colors not in use will be on the wrong side of the piece, facing away from you. When you are crocheting the wrong-side rows, the colors not in use will be facing you.

For large areas of the same color, it is best to attach small balls of yarn (of the changing color) on each side of the large area instead of working over the color.

Rooster Table Runner
Chart

Table Runner

Row 1 (RS): With cloud, ch 55 *(not too loosely)*, sc in 2nd ch from hook and in each rem ch across, turn. *(54 sc)*

Rows 2–4: Ch 1, sc in each sc across, turn.

Row 5 (RS): Ch 1, sc in first 31 sc, in last st **change color to mustard** *(see Pattern Notes, illustration and Chart)*, sc in next sc, in last st change color to cloud, sc in rem 22 sc, turn. *(31 cloud sc, 1 mustard sc, 22 cloud sc)*

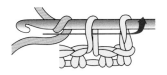

Single Crochet Color Change

Note: For best results, join a small ball of dove on each side of the rooster feet for the grass stems starting in the next row.

Row 6 (WS): Ch 1, sc in first 4 sc, change color to dove, sc in next 5 sc, change color to cloud, sc in next sc, change color to dove, sc in next 2 sc, change color to cloud, sc in next 10 sc, change color to mustard, sc in next 2 sc, change color to cloud, sc in next 12 sc, change color to dove, sc in next 5 sc, change color to cloud, sc in next 3 sc, change color to dove, sc in next 4 sc, change color to cloud, sc in rem 6 sc, turn. *(4 cloud sc, 5 dove sc, 1 cloud sc, 2 dove sc, 10 cloud sc,*

2 mustard sc, 12 cloud sc, 5 dove sc, 3 cloud sc, 4 dove sc, 6 cloud sc)

Rows 7–62: Referring to **Chart** (see Pattern Notes and Chart) for color changes, ch 1, sc in each sc across, turn.

Fasten off all colors except cloud.

Rows 63–232: With cloud, ch 1, sc in each sc across, turn.

Note: For 2nd rooster, turn Chart upside down and read from the top (row 62) down, until row 1 of rooster has been completed.

Rows 233 & 234 (beg Chart): With cloud, ch 1, sc in each sc across, turn.

Row 235 (RS): Following row 60 of Chart, ch 1, sc in first 42 sc, change color to graphite, sc in next sc, change color to cloud, sc in rem 11 sc, turn. (42 cloud sc, 1 graphite sc, 11 cloud sc)

Row 236 (WS): Following row 59 of Chart, ch 1, sc in first 11 sc, change color to graphite, sc in next 2 sc, change color to cloud, sc in rem 41 sc, turn. (11 cloud sc, 2 graphite sc, 41 cloud sc)

Rows 237–294: Referring to Chart for color changes, ch 1, sc in each sc across, turn.

Fasten off all colors except cloud.

Border

Rnd 1 (RS): With cloud, ch 1, 2 sc in first sc, sc in next 52 sc, 3 sc in last sc (for corner), rotate Table Runner to work across left edge, evenly place 292 sc down left edge, rotate to work across underside of foundation ch, 3 sc in first ch, sc in next 52 chs, 3 sc in last ch, rotate to work across right edge, evenly place 292 sc up right edge, 1 sc in same st as beg 2 sc to complete corner, **join** (see Pattern Notes) to beg sc, do not turn. Fasten off. (700 sc)

Place a st marker in the 2nd sc of each corner.

Rnd 2 (RS): Join snow in any marked sc, ch 1, *3 sc in marked sc, [sc in **back lp** (see Stitch Guide) of next sc, sc in next sc] to next marked st; rep from * around, join in beg sc. Fasten off.

Finishing

If needed, do any touch-up embroidery. Weave in loose ends. With graphite, embroider a **French knot** (see illustration) for each rooster's eye using photo as a guide. ●

French Knot

Kitty's Carrot

Design by Lindsey Stephens

Skill Level

 EASY

Finished Measurement

7 inches long

Materials

3 LIGHT

- Red Heart Designer Sport light (DK) weight yarn (3 oz/279 yds/ 85g per ball):
  28 yds each #3251 melon and #3650 pistachio
- Size H/8/5mm crochet hook or size needed to obtain gauge
- Tapestry needle
- Knee-high stocking
- 2 oz catnip

Gauge

4 sc = 1 inch; 5 sc rnds = 1 inch

Pattern Notes

Weave in loose ends as work progresses.

Join rounds with a slip stitch unless otherwise stated.

Cut 6-inch section, including foot, from knee-high stocking. Fill with catnip and tie opening closed.

Special Stitch

Leaf stitch (leaf st): Ch 4, sc in 2nd ch from hook, sc in each of next 2 chs.

Carrot

Leaf Branch
Make 3.

Row 1: With pistachio, ch 15, sl st in 2nd ch from hook, [sl st in each of next 3 chs, **leaf st** *(see Special Stitch)*, sl st in same ch as leaf st, hold the yarn in front of the foundation ch and rotate foundation ch 180 degrees, move yarn back to normal position, leaf st, keeping yarn behind foundation ch rotate foundation ch 180 degrees back to starting position, sl st in next ch of foundation ch] 3 times, sl st in last ch, fasten off, but do not weave in ends. *(6-leaf st)*

Carrot Root

Rnd 1: With melon, ch 2, 6 sc in 2nd ch from hook, **join** *(see Pattern Notes)* in beg sc. *(6 sc)*

Rnd 2: Ch 1, 2 sc in each sc around, join in beg sc. *(12 sc)*

Rnd 3: Ch 1, sc in first sc, 2 sc in next sc, [sc in next sc, 2 sc in next sc] 5 times, join in beg sc. *(18 sc)*

Rnd 4: Ch 1, [sc in each of next 2 sc, 2 sc in next sc] 6 times, join in beg sc. *(24 sc)*

Rnd 5: Ch 1, sc in each sc around, join in beg sc.

Rnds 6–11: Rep rnd 5.

At this point stop working to attach the leaf bunch. Thread the yarn tails of the leaf branches into your Carrot Root through the hole in the center of beg rnd. Arrange so that only the first ch of the foundation ch is inside the Carrot Root *(the rem should be sticking out the top)*. Weave the yarn ends, including the starting melon end, into the carrot root in order to secure the left branches. You may choose to use a dab of glue for a stronger hold.

Rnd 12: Ch 1, [sc in each of next 2 sc, **sc dec** *(see Stitch Guide)* in next 2 sc] around, join in beg sc. *(18 sc)*

Rnds 13–15: Ch 1, sc in each sc around, join in beg sc.

Insert the catnip stuffing into the Carrot Root working around the stuffing and eventually enclosing it inside.

Rnd 16: Ch 1, [sc in next sc, sc dec in next 2 sc] around, join in beg sc. *(12 sc)*

Rnds 17 & 18: Rep rnd 5.

Rnd 19: Ch 1, [sc dec in next 2 sc] around, join in beg sc. *(6 sc)*

Rnd 20: Rep rnd 5.

Rnd 21: Ch 1, [sc dec in next 2 sc] 3 times, join in beg sc, leaving a 5-inch length of yarn, fasten off.

Weave rem length through rem 3 sts, draw opening closed, knot to secure, fasten off. ●

Cheery Tissue Box Cover

Design by Jennine Korejko

Skill Level

 EASY

Finished Measurements

5 inches wide x 5 inches long x 6 inches tall

Materials

- Berroco Comfort medium (worsted) weight nylon/acrylic yarn (3½ oz/210 yds/100g per skein):
    - 1 oz each #9785 falseberry heather and #9701 ivory
    - 2 yds each 5 scrap colors
- Size I/9/5.5mm crochet hook or size needed to obtain gauge
- Tapestry needle

Gauge

Rnds 1 and 2 = 1½ inches high

Pattern Notes

Weave in loose ends as work progresses.

Join with slip stitch as indicated unless otherwise stated.

Chain-3 at beginning of round counts as a double crochet unless otherwise stated.

Special Stitch

Puff stitch (puff st): [Yo, insert hook in st indicated, yo, draw up lp] twice, yo and draw through all 5 lps on hook.

Cover

Side Square

Make 4.

Rnd 1 (RS): With any scrap color, ch 4, **join** *(see Pattern Notes)* in first ch to form ring, **ch 3** *(see Pattern Notes)*, 15 dc in ring, join in 3rd ch of beg ch-3. Fasten off. *(16 dc)*

Rnd 2: Join scrap color in same ch as joining, ch 3, dc in same ch as beg ch-3, ch 2, (2 dc, ch 3, 2 dc) in same ch as beg ch-3 *(beg corner made)*, ch 2, 2 dc in same ch-3 as beg ch-3, **change color** *(see Stitch Guide)* to next scrap color in last dc, sk next 3 dc, *2 dc in next dc, ch 2, (2 dc, ch 3, 2 dc) in same dc *(corner made)*, ch 2, 2 dc in same dc, change color to next scrap color in last dc, sk next 3 dc, rep from * twice, join in 3rd ch of beg ch-3. Fasten off. *(32 dc)*

Rnd 3: Join ivory in ch-3 sp of any corner, ch 1, (2 sc, ch 2, 2 sc) in same sp as beg ch-1 *(sc corner made)*, 2 sc in next ch-2 sp, ch 1, dc in sp between next two 2-dc groups, ch 1, 2 sc in next ch-2 sp, *(2 sc , ch 2, 2 sc) in next corner ch-3 sp *(sc corner made)*, 2 sc in next ch-2 sp, ch 1, dc in sp between next two 2-dc groups, ch 1, 2 sc in next ch-2 sp, rep from * twice, join in first sc.

Rnd 4: Ch 3, dc in next sc, (dc, ch 2, dc) in next corner ch-2 sp *(dc corner made)*, dc in each of next 4 sc, in next ch-1 sp, in next dc and in next ch-1 sp, *dc in each of next 4 sc, (dc, ch 2, dc) in next corner ch-2 sp *(dc corner made)*, dc in each of next 4 sc, in next ch-1 sp, in next dc and in next ch-1 sp, rep from * twice, dc in each of next 2 sc, join in 3rd ch of beg ch-3. Fasten off. *(52 dc)*

Rnd 5: Hold piece with WS facing you; join ivory in same ch as joining of previous rnd, ch 1, sc in same ch as beg ch-1, [**puff st** *(see Special Stitch)* in next dc, sc in next dc] 3 times, in next corner ch-2 sp work (puff st, ch 2, puff st), *sc in next dc, [puff st in next dc, sc in next dc] 6 times, (puff st, ch 2, puff st) in next corner ch-2 sp, rep from * twice, sc in next dc, puff st in last dc, join in first sc. Fasten off.

Top Square
Rnd 1 (RS): With scrap color, ch 16, join in first ch to form ring, ch 1, working in **back lp** *(see Stitch Guide)*, sc in same ch as joining and in each rem ch around, join in first sc. Fasten off. *(16 sc)*

Rnd 2: Join scrap color in same sc as joining, ch 3, dc in same sc as beg ch-3, ch 2, (2 dc, ch 3, 2 dc) in same sc *(beg corner made)*, ch 2, dc in same sc, change color to next scrap color in last dc, sk next 3 sc, *2 dc in next sc, ch 2, (2 dc, ch 3, 2 dc) in same sc *(corner made)*, ch 2, 2 dc in same sc, change color to next scrap color in last dc, sk next 3 sc, rep from * twice, join in 3rd ch of beg ch-3. Fasten off.

Rnds 3–5: Rep rnds 3–5 of Side Square.

Assembly
Hold 2 Side Squares with WS tog and carefully match sts. With tapestry needle and falseberry heather, and beg and ending in corner sps, sew sides tog along 1 edge. In same manner, sew rem Side Squares tog and sew Top Square to top edges of Side Squares.

Bottom Edging
Rnd 1 (RS): Hold piece with RS facing, join falseberry heather in any st, ch 1, sc in same st, in each rem st and in each corner sp, join in first sc. Fasten off.

Rnd 2 (WS): Hold piece with WS facing you; join ivory in same sc as joining of previous rnd, ch 1, sc in same sc as beg ch-1, puff st in next sc, *sc in next sc, puff st in next sc, rep from * around, join in first sc, **turn**.

Rnd 3 (RS): Ch 1, sc in same sc as beg ch-1, sc in each rem sc around, join in first sc. Fasten off. ●

Sunset Colors Throw

Design by Katherine Eng

Skill Level

 INTERMEDIATE

Finished Measurements

43½ inches wide x 57 inches long

Materials

- Red Heart Super Saver medium (worsted) weight acrylic yarn (5 oz/244 yds/141g per skein):
  7 skeins #942 melonberry
- Size J/10/6mm crochet hook or size needed to obtain gauge
- Tapestry needle

4 MEDIUM

Gauge

Rows 1–5 = 3 inches; 9 sc = 3 inches

Pattern Notes

Weave in loose ends as work progresses.

Chain-6 at beginning of row counts as first double crochet and chain-3 unless otherwise stated.

Chain-4 at beginning of a row or round counts as first double crochet and chain-1 unless otherwise stated.

Join with slip stitch as indicated unless otherwise stated.

Special Stitch

Shell: 7 dc in indicated st.

Throw

Row 1 (WS): Working from top to bottom of Throw, ch 138, working in **back bar of ch** *(see illustration)* sc in 2nd ch from hook, sc in back bar of each rem ch across, turn. *(137 sc)*

Back Bar of Chain

Row 2 (RS): Ch 1, sc in first sc, [sk next 3 sc, **shell** (see Special Stitch) in next sc, sk next 3 sc, sc in next sc] across, turn. *(17 shells, 18 sc)*

Row 3: Ch 6 *(see Pattern Notes)*, *sc in center dc of next shell, ch 3, dc in next sc**, ch 3, rep from * across, ending last rep at **, turn.

Row 4: Ch 4 *(see Pattern Notes)*, *dc in next ch-3 sp, ch 1, dc in next sc, ch 1, dc in next ch-3 sp, ch 1**, dc in next dc, ch 1, rep from * across, ending last rep at **, dc in 3rd ch of beg ch-6, turn.

Row 5: Ch 1, sc in first dc, [ch 1, sk next ch-1 sp, sc in next dc] across, ending with ch 1, sk next ch, sc in 3rd ch of beg ch-4, turn.

Row 6: Ch 1, sc in first sc, [sk next ch-1 sp, next sc and next ch-1 sp, shell in next sc, sk next ch-1 sp, next sc and next ch-1 sp, sc in next sc] across, turn.

Rows 7–90: [Rep rows 3–6 consecutively] 21 times.

Row 91: Rep row 3.

Row 92: Ch 1, sc in first dc, [3 sc in ch-3 sp, sc in next sc, 3 sc in next ch-3 sp, sc in next dc] across, **do not turn**. *(137 sc)*

Border

Rnd 1 (RS): Working across edge, work 3 sc over post of each dc on edge and sc in end of each sc at end of row, ending with (sc, ch 2, sc) through 2 lps of corner ch, sc through 2 lps of each ch across foundation ch, ending with (sc, ch 2, sc) in last ch, working across opposite edge of Throw, work 3 sc over post of each dc on edge and sc in end of each sc at end of row, ending with (sc, ch 2, sc) in corner sc, sc in each sc across, ending with (sc, ch 2, sc) in last sc, **join** *(see Pattern Notes)* in beg sc. *(183 sc each side between corner ch-2 sps; 137 sc top and bottom)*

Rnd 2 (RS): Ch 1, sc in first sc, [ch 1, sk next sc, sc in next sc] around, working at each corner, ch 1, sk next sc, (sc, ch 2, sc) in corner ch-2 sp, ending with ch 1, sk last sc, join in beg sc, sl st in next ch-1 sp.

Rnd 3 (RS): Ch 4, sk next sc, dc in next ch-1 sp, [ch 1, sk next sc, dc in next ch-1 sp] around, working in each corner, ch 1, sk next sc, ([dc, ch 1, dc] 3 times, dc) in corner ch-2 sp, ending with ch 1, sk next sc, join to 3rd ch of beg ch-4, turn.

Rnd 4 (WS): Ch 1, sc in next ch-1 sp, [ch 1, sk next dc, sc in next ch-1 sp] around, working in each corner in center ch-1 sp, ch 1, sk next dc, (sc, ch 2, sc) in center corner ch-1 sp, ending with ch 1, sk last dc, join in beg sc, turn, sl st in next ch-1 sp and in next sc.

Rnd 5 (RS): Ch 1, sc in same sc as beg ch-1, [sk next 3 sts *(ch-1 sp, sc and next ch-1 sp)*, shell in next sc, sk next 3 sts *(ch-1 sp, sc and next ch-1 sp)*, sc in next sc] around, working at corners 1 and 3, shell in corner ch-2 sp, sc in next sc, at corners 2 and 4, sk next ch-1 sp and next sc, shell in corner ch-2 sp, sc in next sc, ending with sk last 3 sts, join in beg sc.

Rnd 6 (RS): Ch 1, sc in same sc, *ch 1, sk next dc, sc in next dc, ch 1, sk next dc, (sc, ch 2, sc) in next dc, ch 1, sk next dc, sc in next dc, ch 1, sk next dc**, sc in next sc*, rep from * to * around, working at each corner ch 1, sk next dc, sc in next dc, ch 1, sk 1 dc, (sc, ch 2, sc, ch 3, sc, ch 2, sc) in next dc, ch 1, sk next dc, sc in next dc, ch 1, sk next dc, sc in next sc, ending last rep at **, join in beg sc. Fasten off.

With WS facing, block lightly. ●

Star Flowers Baby Blanket

Design by Rena V. Stevens

Skill Level

 EASY

Finished Measurements

Approximately 36 inches wide x 40 inches long

Materials

- Cascade Anthem medium (worsted) weight acrylic yarn (3½ oz/186 yds/100g per skein):
  - 3 skeins #08 white
  - 1 skein each #03 red, #02 coral and #20 yellow
- Size J/10/6mm crochet hook or size needed to obtain gauge
- Tapestry needle

4 MEDIUM

Gauge

17 dc = 6 inches

Rows 5 & 6 = 1½ inches long

Pattern Notes

Work lengthwise from side edge to side edge.

Edging is created as work progresses.

Some rows may seem too tight until subsequent rows have been worked.

Make color changes by fastening off old color and joining new color with slip stitch in beginning half double crochet of next row.

Eye of stitch is the chain stitch made following completion of flower bottom. When working back across a row of flower bottoms, the eye will be the chain stitch immediately before the top of the flower bottom. Insert hook under front and back loops of eye to work into the chain stitch and not the chain space.

Special Stitches

Bottom petal: In indicated st, yo, insert hook, yo, pull up a lp, yo, draw elongated lp (approximately ½ inch long) through 1 lp on hook.

Picot: Ch 3, with back bar of chs facing, insert hook under back bar and top lp of 3rd ch from hook, yo, pull up lp, yo, draw through both lps on hook.

Petal stitch (petal st): In indicated eye, yo, insert hook, yo, pull up a lp, yo, draw elongated lp (approximately ½ inch long) through 1 lp on hook, yo, draw through all 3 lps on hook.

Flower top: (Petal st—see Special Stitches, ch 2, petal st) in indicated eye.

Alternate picot (alt picot): Ch 3, with back bar of chs facing away, insert hook under back lp and back bar of 3rd ch from hook, yo, pull up lp, yo, draw through both lps on hook.

Blanket

With white, ch 185.

Row 1 (RS): With **back bar of chs** *(see illustration)* facing away, insert hook under back lp and back bar of ch sts, work **bottom petal** *(see Special Stitches)* in 5th ch from hook *(sk chs count as ch sp)* (3 lps on hook), sk next 3 chs, bottom petal in next ch *(5 lps on hook)*, yo, draw through all lps on hook (***flower bottom completed**—see Pattern Notes)*, *ch 3, bottom petal in next ch, sk next 3 chs, bottom petal in next ch, yo, draw through all lps on hook; rep from * across to last ch, ch 2, dc in last ch st, turn. *(36 flower bottoms, 35 ch-3 sps, 1 ch-4 sp, 1 ch-2 sp, 1 dc)*

Front Loop Back Loop

Back Bar

Anatomy of a Chain

Row 2: Picot *(see Special Stitches)*, ch 1, **flower top** *(see Special Stitches)* in each **eye** *(see Pattern Notes)* across, ch 1, hdc in 3rd ch of turn ch, turn. *(36 flower tops, 2 ch-1 sps, 1 picot, 1 hdc)*

Row 3: Picot, ch 3, sk first hdc, work bottom petal in next ch st, sk next petal st, bottom petal in next petal st, yo, draw through all lps on hook, ch 3, *2 dc in next flower top ch-2 sp**, dc in gap between flower tops, rep from * across, ending last rep at ** in second-to-last flower top, ch 3, bottom petal in last petal st of same flower top, sk next petal st, bottom petal in next petal st, yo, draw through all lps on hook ch 3, hdc in next ch st, leave picot unworked, turn. *(101 dc, 2 flower bottoms, 4 ch-3 sps, 1 picot, 1 hdc)*

Row 4: Picot, ch 1, flower top in next eye, ch 1, dc in next and each dc across, flower top in next eye, ch 1, sk next 3 sts, hdc in next ch st, leave picot unworked, fasten off, turn. *(101 dc, 2 flower tops, 3 ch-1 sps, 1 picot, 1 hdc)*

Note: Use flower colors consecutively in the following sequence: red, coral, yellow.

Row 5: With **next flower color** *(see Pattern Notes)*, **alt picot** *(see Special Stitches)*, ch 3, bottom petal in next ch st, sk next petal st, bottom petal in next petal st, yo, draw through all lps on hook, *ch 3, bottom petal in same st as last bottom petal made, sk next 2 dc**, bottom petal in next dc, yo, draw through all lps on hook; rep from * across to last 2 dc; rep once from * to **, bottom petal in next ch st, yo, draw through all lps on hook, ch 3, bottom petal in same st as last bottom petal made, sk next petal st, bottom petal in next petal st, yo, draw through all lps on hook, ch 3, hdc in next ch st, leave picot unworked, turn. *(36 flower bottoms, 37 ch-3 sps, 1 picot, 1 hdc)*

Row 6: Picot, ch 1, flower top in each eye across, ch 1, sk next 3 sts, hdc in next ch st, leave picot unworked, fasten off, turn. *(36 flower tops, 2 ch-1 sps, 1 picot, 1 hdc)*

Row 7: With white, alt picot, ch 3, sk first hdc, work bottom petal in next ch st, sk next petal st, bottom petal in next petal st, yo, draw through all lps on hook, ch 3, *2 dc in next flower top ch-2 sp**, dc in gap between flower tops, rep from * across, ending last rep at ** in second-to-last flower top sp, ch 3, bottom petal in last petal st of same flower top, sk next petal st, bottom petal in next petal st, yo, draw through all lps on hook, ch 3, hdc in next ch st, leave picot unworked, turn. *(101 dc, 2 flower bottoms, 4 ch-3 sps, 1 picot, 1 hdc)*

Rows 8–55: [Rep rows 4–7] 12 more times. *(14 flower strips including beg edge)*

Row 56: Rep row 4 except do not fasten off white.

Row 57: Continuing with white, picot, ch 3, sk first hdc, bottom petal in next ch st, sk next petal st, bottom petal in next petal st, yo, draw through all lps on hook, *ch 3, bottom petal in same st as last bottom petal made, sk next 2 dc**, bottom petal in next dc, yo, draw through all lps on hook; rep from * across to last 2 dc; rep once from * to **, bottom petal in next ch st, yo, draw through all lps on hook, ch 3, bottom petal in same st as last bottom petal made, sk next petal st, bottom petal in next petal st, yo, draw through all lps on hook, ch 3, hdc in next ch st, leave picot unworked, turn. *(36 flower bottoms, 37 ch-3 sps, 1 picot, 1 hdc)*

Row 58: Ch 3, (petal st, ch 3, petal st) in each eye across, sk next 3 sts, dc in next ch st, leave picot unworked. Fasten off. *(36 flower tops, 1 ch-3 sp, 1 dc)*

Tassels

Wrap yarn 16 times around a 4½-inch piece of cardboard. Before cutting, pull a 14-inch length of yarn through top of tassel, tie it tightly, then cut bottom of tassel strands *(A)*. Keeping top tie ends free, wrap another 14-inch length of yarn 3 times around tassel approximately ½ inch from top and tie tightly, leaving tails to become part of tassel *(B)*. Pull one top tie tail through end flower at corner of blanket and tie to second tail. Use needle to thread all yarn tails down through tassel.

Rep for rem 3 corners of blanket. Trim tassel ends evenly. ●

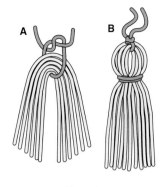

Tassel

Stripes
Microwave Bowl Cozy

Design by Agnes Russell

Skill Level

 ■■□□ EASY

Finished Size

Fits 8-oz microwavable glass dish

Finished Measurement

4¼ inches in diameter

Gauge

Rnds 1–5 = 3 inches in diameter

Pattern Notes

Join with slip stitch as indicated unless otherwise stated.

Do not turn rounds unless otherwise indicated.

Bowl Cozy

Rnd 1 (RS): Ch 6, **join** *(see Pattern Notes)* in first ch to form a ring, ch 1, 10 sc in ring, join in beg sc, **do not turn rnds** *(see Pattern Notes)*. *(10 sc)*

Rnd 2: Ch 1, 2 sc in each sc around, join in beg sc. *(20 sc)*

Rnd 3: Ch 1, [sc in next sc, 2 sc in next sc] around, join in beg sc. *(30 sc)*

Rnd 4: Ch 1, [2 sc in next sc, sc in each of next 2 sc] around, join in beg sc. *(40 sc)*

Rnd 5: Ch 1, [sc in each of next 9 sc, 2 sc in next sc] 4 times, join in beg sc. *(44 sc)*

Rnds 6–9: Ch 1, sc in each sc around, join in beg sc.

Rnd 10: Ch 1, sc in first sc, ch 2, sk next sc, [sc in next sc, ch 2, sk next sc] around, join in beg sc. *(22 sc, 22 ch-2 sps)*

Rnds 11–13: Sl st in next ch-2 sp, ch 1, sc in same ch-2 sp, [ch 2, sc in next ch-2 sp] around, join in beg sc. *(22 sc, 22 ch-2 sps)*

Rnd 14: Sl st in next ch-2 sp, ch 1, 2 sc in same ch-2 sp, *(sc, dc, tr) in next ch-2 sp, 3 tr in next ch-2 sp, (tr, dc, sc) in next ch-2 sp (handle)*, 2 sc in each of next 8 ch-2 sps, rep from * to * once, 2 sc in each of next 7 ch-2 sps, join in beg sc, **turn.** *(4 dc, 10 tr, 36 sc)*

Rnd 15 (WS): Ch 1, **reverse sc** *(see Stitch Guide)* in each st around, join in beg ch 1. Fasten off.

Weave in ends with tapestry needle. ●

Bumble Buzz Purse

Design by Sadonna Schwab

Skill Level

 **EASY**

Finished Measurements

6¾ inches wide x 9 inches long, plus Wings and Antennae

Materials

- Bernat Super Value medium (worsted) weight acrylic yarn (7 oz/426 yds/197g per skein):
   5 oz #307421 black
   3 oz #300608 bright yellow
   1 oz #307414 natural
- Size 7/4.5mm crochet hook or size needed to obtain gauge
- Tapestry needle
- 22mm black shank buttons: 2

Gauge

7 sc rows = 1½ inches; 7 sc = 1½ inches

Pattern Notes

Weave in loose ends as work progresses.

Join with slip stitch as indicated unless otherwise stated.

Purse

Front Body

Row 1 (RS): Beg at bottom of Front Body, with natural, ch 10, 2 sc in 2nd ch from hook, [sk 1 ch, 2 sc in next ch] 4 times, turn. *(10 sc)*

Row 2: Ch 1, 2 sc in first sc, [sk 1 sc, 2 sc in next sc] 4 times, 2 sc in last sc, **change color** *(see Stitch Guide)* to black, fasten off natural, turn. *(12 sc)*

Row 3: Ch 1, 2 sc in first sc, [sk next sc, 2 sc in next sc] across to last sc, 2 sc in last sc, turn. *(14 sc)*

Rows 4–6: Rep row 3. At the end of row 6, change color to yellow, fasten off black. *(20 sc)*

Rows 7 & 8: Rep row 3. *(24 sc)*

Row 9: Ch 1, sc in first sc, [sk next sc, 2 sc in next sc] across to last sc, sc in last sc, turn. *(24 sc)*

Row 10: Rep row 9, change color to black, fasten off yellow, turn.

Rows 11 & 12: Rep row 9. At the end of row 12, change color to yellow, fasten off black, turn.

Rows 13–16: Rep row 9. At the end of row 16, change color to black, fasten off yellow, turn.

Rows 17 & 18: Rep row 9. At the end of row 18, change color to yellow, fasten off black, turn.

Row 19: Rep row 9.

Rows 20–22: Ch 1, **sc dec** *(see Stitch Guide)* in next 2 sc, [sk next sc, 2 sc in next sc] across to last 2 sc, sc dec in last 2 sc, turn. At the end of row 22, change color to black, fasten off yellow, turn. *(18 sc)*

Rows 23–25: Ch 1, sc in first sc, [sk next sc, 2 sc in next sc] across, sc in last sc, turn. At the end of row 25, fasten off. *(18 sc)*

Back Body

Rows 1–24: Rep rows 1–24 of Front Body.

Row 25: Ch 1, sc in first sc, [sk next sc, 2 sc in next sc] across, sc in last sc, turn. *(18 sc)*

Row 26: Rep row 25.

Rows 27–30: Ch 1, sc dec in next 2 sc, [sk next sc, 2 sc in next sc] across to last 2 sc, sc dec in last 2 sc, turn. *(10 sc)*

Row 31: Working in **back lp** *(see Stitch Guide)* only, ch 1, sc in first st, [sk next sc, 2 sc in next st] 4 times, sc in last st, turn. *(10 sc)*

Row 32: Ch 1, 2 sc in first sc, [sk next sc, 2 sc in next sc] 4 times, 2 sc in last st, turn. *(12 sc)*

Rows 33–35: Ch 1, 2 sc in first sc, [sk next sc, 2 sc in next sc] across, ending with 2 sc in last sc, turn. *(18 sc)*

Rows 36 & 37: Rep row 25.

Row 38: Ch 1, sc in first sc, [sk next sc, 2 sc in next sc] twice, [ch 2, sk next 3 sc *(buttonhole)*, 2 sc in next, sk next sc, 2 sc in next] twice, 1 sc in last sc, turn. *(14 sc, 2 ch-2 sps)*

Row 39: Ch 1, sc in first sc, [sk next sc, 2 sc in next sc] twice, 2 sc in ch-2 sp, sk next sc, 2 sc in next sc, sk 1 sc, 2 sc in next sc, 2 sc in next ch-2 sp, [sk next sc, 2 sc in next sc] twice, sc in last sc. Fasten off.

Gusset

First Side

Row 1: With natural, ch 4, sc in 2nd ch from hook, sc in each of next 2 chs, turn. *(3 sc)*

Row 2: Ch 1, sc in each sc across, turn.

Rows 3–13: Rep row 2. At the end of last rep, change color to black.

Rows 14–17: Rep row 2. At the end of last rep, change color to yellow.

Rows 18–21: Rep row 2. At the end of last rep, change color to black.

Rows 22 & 23: Rep row 2. At the end of last rep, change color to yellow.

Rows 24–27: Rep row 2. At the end of last rep, change color to black.

Rows 28 & 29: Rep row 2. At the end of last rep, change color to yellow.

Rows 30–33: Rep row 2. At the end of last rep, change color to black.

Shoulder Strap

[Ch 1, sc in each of next 3 sc, turn] to desired length of Shoulder Strap. At the end of last row, change color to yellow.

2nd Side

Rows 34–37: Rep row 2. At the end of last rep, change color to black.

Rows 38 & 39: Rep row 2. At the end of last rep, change color to yellow.

Rows 40–43: Rep row 2. At the end of last rep, change color to black.

Rows 44 & 45: Rep row 2. At the end of last rep, change color to yellow.

Rows 46–49: Rep row 2. At the end of last rep, change color to black.

Rows 50–53: Rep row 2.

At the end of last rep, with care that Gusset and Shoulder Strap are not twisted, with WS facing, working through both thicknesses of row 53 and opposite side of foundation ch of row 1, sl st in each st across. Fasten off.

Antenna
Make 2.

Row 1: With black, ch 13, [yo, insert hook in 4th ch from hook, yo, draw up a lp, yo, draw through 2 lps on hook] 3 times, yo, draw through all 4 lps on hook, sl st in each of next 9 chs, leaving 8-inch length of yarn, fasten off.

Large Upper Wing
Make 2.

With natural, ch 10, 3 dc in 4th ch from hook (3 sk chs count as first dc), dc in each of next 2 chs, hdc in next ch, sc in each of next 2 chs, sl st in last ch, working on opposite side of foundation ch, sc in each of next 2 chs, hdc in next ch, dc in each of next 2 chs, 4 dc in same ch as beg dc sts, **join** (see Pattern Notes) in 3rd ch of beg dc. Fasten off.

Small Lower Wing
Make 2.

With natural, ch 8, 2 hdc in 3rd ch from hook (2 sk chs count as first hdc), hdc in next ch, sc in each of next 3 chs, sl st in last ch, working on opposite side of foundation ch, sc in each of next 3 chs, hdc in next ch, 3 hdc in same ch as beg dc sts, join in 2nd ch of beg hdc. Fasten off.

Assembly

With RS tog, matching colors, **whipstitch edges** (see illustration) of Gusset to Front Body. Matching sts of Back Body to opposite edge of Gusset, whipstitch edges tog.

Whipstitch Edges

Sew Antennae centered to top of row 31 of Purse, just in front of rem free lps of row 31. Sew buttons for eyes centered over rows 24 and 25 of Front Body in line with buttonholes.

Sew Wings to Gusset on each side of Body centered over center strip of yellow. ●

Made-to-Fit Mittens

Design by Kristen Stoltzfus Clay

Skill Level

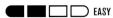 EASY

Finished Size

Instructions given fit 7-inch-long hand.

Finished Measurement

9 inches long, including Wrist Skirt

Materials

- Cascade Yarns Baby Alpaca Chunky bulky (chunky) weight baby alpaca yarn (3½ oz/108 yds/ 100g per hank):
    1 hank each #624 blue/gray mix and #562 blue
- Size K/10½/6.50mm crochet hook or size needed to obtain gauge
- Stitch markers
- Tapestry needle

Gauge

Rnds 1–3 = 1½ inches in diameter

Pattern Notes

This pattern is customizable to the wearer's hand. Round 7 is repeated as needed until Mitten hand reaches base of thumb.

Do not join or turn unless otherwise stated.

Mark beginning of each round.

Make sure that round 7 on both mittens is exactly the same.

Special Stitches

Beginning shell (beg shell): (Ch 3, dc, ch 2, 2 dc) in indicated st.

Shell: (2 dc, ch 2, 2 dc) in indicated st.

Picot: Ch 3, sl st in indicated st.

Beginning picot shell (beg picot shell): (Ch 3, 2 dc, **picot**—*see Special Stitches*, 2 dc) in indicated sp.

Picot shell: (3 dc, picot, 2 dc) in indicated sp.

Mitten

Make 2.

Hand

Rnd 1: With blue/gray mix, ch 3, 2 sc in 2nd ch from hook, 2 sc in next ch, working in rem lps on opposite side of ch, 2 sc in rem lp of each of next 2 chs, **do not join or turn** *(see Pattern Notes). (8 sc)*

Rnd 2: [Sc in next sc, 2 sc in next sc] 4 times. *(12 sc)*

Rnd 3: [2 sc in next sc, sc in each of next 5 sc] twice. *(14 sc)*

Rnd 4: [2 sc in each of next 2 sc, sc in each of next 5 sc] twice. *(18 sc)*

Rnd 5: Sc in next sc, 2 sc in each of next 2 sc, sc in each of next 7 sc, 2 sc in each of next 2 sc, sc in each of next 6 sc. *(22 sc)*

Rnd 6: Sc in each of next 2 sc, 2 sc in each of next 2 sts, sc in each of next 9 sc, 2 sc in each of next 2 sts, sc in each of next 7 sc. *(26 sc)*

Rnd 7: Sc in each sc around.

Next rnds: Rep rnd 7 until Hand is 1 rnd short of base of wearer's thumb.

Left-Hand Mitten
Last rnd: Rep rnd 7, ending on outside of thumb, **do not fasten off**.

Right-Hand Mitten
Last rnd: Rep rnd 7, ending on inside of thumb, ending last rep with last st on outside of thumb, **do not fasten off**, **turn**.

For Both Mittens

Thumb Shaping
Row 1: Ch 1, sc in each sc around, turn. *(26 sc)*

Row 2: Ch 1, sc in first sc, **sc dec** in next 2 sc, sc in each sc around to last 2 sts, sc dec in last 2 sc, turn. *(24 sc)*

Row 3: Ch 1, sc in each sc around, turn.

Row 4: Ch 1, 2 sc in first sc, sc in each sc around to last sc, 2 sc in last sc, turn. *(26 sc)*

Note: Try on Mitten at this point. If Thumb Shaping is too tight, rep row 3 once, do not turn.

Row 5: Rep row 4, join with sl st in first sc, **do not turn**. *(28 sc)*

Wrist
Rnd 1: With RS facing, ch 1, [sc in each of next 12 sc, sc dec in next 2 sts] twice, **do not join**. *(26 sc)*

Rnd 2: [Sc in each of next 11 sc, sc dec in next 2 sts] twice. *(24 sc)*

Rnd 3: [Sc in each of next 10 sc, sc dec in next 2 sts] twice, join in next st. Fasten off. *(22 sc)*

Wrist Skirt
Rnd 1: With RS facing, join blue in any sc of rnd 3 of Wrist, [sc in each of next 9 sc, sc dec in next 2 sts] twice, **do not join**. *(20 sc)*

Rnd 2: Sc in each sc around.

Rnd 3: Rep rnd 2, join in first sc.

Rnd 4: Beg shell *(see Special Stitches)* in same st as join, ch 1, sk next sc, sc in next sc, ch 1, sk next sc, [**shell** *(see Special Stitches)* in next sc, ch 1, sk next sc, sc in next sc, ch 1, sk next sc] around, join in beg ch-3. *(5 shells, 5 sc)*

Rnd 5: Sl st across to ch-2 sp of next shell, sl st in ch-2 sp, **beg picot shell** *(see Special Stitches)* in same sp as last sl st, dc in next sc, **picot** *(see Special Stitches)* in dc just made, [**picot shell** *(see Special Stitches)* in ch-2 sp of next shell, dc in next sc, picot in dc just made] around, join in beg ch-3. Fasten off. *(5 picot shells, 5 dc, 5 picot)*

Thumb
Rnd 1: With RS facing, join blue in end of any Thumb Shaping row, 14 sc evenly sp around opening left by Thumb Shaping, **do not join**.

Rnds 2 & 3: Sc in each sc around. *(14 sc)*

Rnd 4: [Sc dec in next 2 sc, sc in each of next 5 sc] twice. *(12 sc)*

Rnd 5: [Sc dec in next 2 sc, sc in each of next 4 sc] twice. *(10 sc)*

Rnd 6: Sc in each sc around.

Rnds 7 & 8: Rep rnd 6.

Note: Try on Mitten at this point. If Thumb needs to be longer, rep rnd 6 to add length. If Thumb needs to be shorter, pull out rows to desired length.

Rnd 9: [Sc dec in next 2 sts, sc in each of next 3 sc] twice. *(8 sc)*

Rnd 10: [Sc dec, sc in each of next 2 sc] twice. *(6 sc)*

Rnd 11: [Sc dec in next 2 sts] around. *(3 sc)*

Rnd 12: Sk next sc, sl st in next sc. Leaving rem sc unworked, fasten off.

Finishing

Weave in ends. With blue and **straight stitch** *(see illustration)*, embroider sts on RS rows for Thumb Shaping. ●

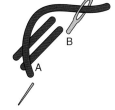

Straight Stitch

Bear & Lion Trinket Holders

Designs by Kathleen Stuart

Skill Level

 EASY

Finished Measurements

4½ inches wide x 1 inch tall on sides

Materials

- Red Heart Super Saver medium (worsted) weight acrylic yarn (7 oz/364 yds/198g per skein):
    1 skein #326 oatmeal
    2 yds #312 black
- Size G/6/4mm crochet hook or size needed to obtain gauge
- Fiberfill
- 6mm black animal eyes: 4
- Tapestry needle
- Stitch marker

4 MEDIUM

Gauge

5 sc = 1 inch; 4 sc rnds = 2 inches; 5 hdc rnds = 4 inches

Pattern Notes

Each trinket holders require 2 ounces oatmeal.

Weave in loose ends as work progresses.

Work in rounds; do not join and do not turn unless otherwise indicated.

Join with slip stitch as indicated unless otherwise stated.

Chain-2 at beginning of round counts as first half double crochet unless otherwise stated.

Special Stitches

Loop stitch (lp st): Wrap yarn from front to back over index finger *(2 strands on finger)*, insert hook in indicated st, pick up lower strand and pull up a lp *(2 lps on hook)*, yo and draw working yarn through both lps. Push lp off finger.

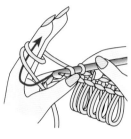

Loop Stitch (2 loops)

Single crochet join (sc join): Place a slip knot on hook *(see illustration A)*, insert hook in indicated st, yo, pull up a lp *(see illustration B)*, yo and draw through both lps on hook *(see illustration C).*

A

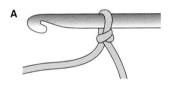

B

C

Single Crochet Join

Trinket Holders

Bear Head

Rnd 1: With oatmeal, ch 2, 6 sc in 2nd ch from hook, **do not join or turn** *(see Pattern Notes)*. *(6 sc)*

Rnd 2: Sc in each sc around.

Rnd 3: Working in **back lps** *(see Stitch Guide)*, 2 sc in each st around. *(12 sc)*

Rnd 4: [Sc in next sc, 2 sc in next sc] around. *(18 sc)*

Rnd 5: [Sc in next 2 sc, 2 sc in next sc] around. *(24 sc)*

Rnd 6: Working in back lps, sc in next 10 sts, working in **front lp** *(see Stitch Guide)*, (sl st, **ch 2**— *see Pattern Notes*, 2 hdc, ch 2, sl st) in next st *(for ear)*, working in back lps, sc in each of next 4 sts, working in front lp, (sl st, ch 2, 2 hdc, ch 2, sl st) in next st *(for ear)*, working in back lps, sc in each of next 8 sts. *(22 sc, 8 hdc)*

Rnd 7: [Sc in each of next 2 sc, **sc dec** *(see Stitch Guide)* in next 2 sts] twice, sc in next 2 sts, sk ear sts, sc in next 4 sc, sk ear sts, [sc in next 2 sc, sc dec in next 2 sc] twice. *(18 sc)*

Rnd 8: [Sc in next sc, sc dec in next 2 sc] around. Sew eyes between rnds 3 and 4, leaving 1 sc between eyes. Stuff head. *(12 sc)*

Rnd 9: [Sc dec in next 2 sc] 6 times, sl st in next st, leaving an 8-inch length of yarn, fasten off. *(6 sc)*

Lion Head

Rnds 1–5: Rep rnds 1–5 of Bear Head. *(24 sc)*

Rnd 6: Sl st in next st, turn, working in front lps, **lp st** *(see Special Stitches)* in next 8 sts, working in back lp, (sl st, ch 2, 2 hdc, ch 2, sl st) in next st *(for ear)*, working in front lps, lp st in next 4 sts, working in back lp, (sl st, ch 2, 2 hdc, ch 2, sl st) in next st *(for ear)*, working in front lps, lp st in next 10 sts, **join** *(see Pattern Notes)* in first st, turn. *(22 lp sts, 8 hdc)*

Rnds 7–9: Rep rnds 7–9 of Bear Head. *(6 sc)*

Base
Make 2.

Rnd 1: With oatmeal, ch 3, 9 hdc in 3rd ch from hook, join in first hdc. *(10 hdc)*

Rnd 2: Ch 2, hdc in same st as beg ch-2, 2 hdc in each hdc around, join in beg ch-2. *(20 hdc)*

Rnd 3: Ch 2, 2 hdc in next hdc, [hdc in next hdc, 2 hdc in next hdc] around, join in top of beg ch-2. *(30 hdc)*

Rnd 4: Ch 2, hdc in next hdc, 2 hdc in next hdc, [hdc in next 2 hdc, 2 hdc in next hdc] around, join in top of beg ch-2. *(40 hdc)*

Rnd 5: Ch 2, hdc in next 2 hdc, 2 hdc in next hdc, [hdc in next 3 hdc, 2 hdc in next hdc] around, join in top of beg ch-2. *(50 hdc)*

Rnd 6: Ch 2, working in back lps only, hdc in each st around, join in beg ch-2. *(50 hdc)*

Rnd 7: Ch 2, hdc in each hdc around, join in beg ch-2. Fasten off. *(50 hdc)*

Joining Head

Working in rem front lps of rnd 5, with side of base facing, **sc join** *(see Special Stitches)* in first st, sc in each of next 2 sts, ch 6, dc in 3rd ch from hook, dc in next 3 chs, sk next 2 sts on rnd 5, sc in next 13 sts *(for first leg)*, ch 6, dc in 3rd ch from hook, dc in next 3 chs, sk next 2 sts, sc in next 2 sts *(for 2nd leg)*, place back of head next to side of base, working in both front lps of last st of rnd 6 of head and next st on base, sc in next st, sc in next 4 sts of head and base, sc in next st of body only, ch 6, dc in 3rd ch from hook, dc in next 3 chs sk next 2 sts, sc in next 13 sts *(for 3rd leg)*, ch 6, dc in 3rd ch from hook, dc in next 3 chs sk next 2 sts, sc in each of next 3 sts *(for 4th leg)*, (sc, dc, ch 2, sl st) in last st *(for bear tail)*, (sc, ch 8, sc in 2nd ch from hook, sc in each of next 6 chs, sl st) in last st *(for lion tail)*, for both sl st in beg sc. Fasten off.

Finishing

With a length of black, embroider nose with **triangle satin stitch** *(see illustration)* over rnd 1 and embroider mouth with **outline stitch** *(see illustration)* on rnd 2 of head centered below nose. Fasten off. ●

Triangle Satin Stitch

Outline Stitch

Cozy Slipper Socks

Design by Jackie Daugherty

Skill Level

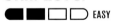 EASY

Finished Sizes

Instructions given fit woman's size small; changes for medium and large are in [ ].

Finished Measurements

Foot Length: 8½ inches *(small)* [9½ inches *(medium)*, 10½ inches *(large)*]

Leg Length: 8 inches

Materials

- Plymouth Yarn Encore Chunky Tweed bulky (chunky) weight acrylic/wool/rayon yarn (3½ oz/ 143 yds/100g per ball):
  - 2 balls #4108 medium blue
- Plymouth Yarn Encore Chunky bulky (chunky) weight acrylic/wool yarn (3½ oz/143 yds/ 100g per ball):
  - 1 ball #0240 taupe
- Size L/11/8mm crochet hook or size needed to obtain gauge
- Tapestry needle
- Pompom maker (optional)

Gauge

9 hdc = 4 inches; 8 rows = 4 inches in half double crochet

11 sc = 4 inches; 13 rows = 4 inches in single crochet

Pattern Notes

Weave in loose ends as work progresses.

When one set of numbers is given, it applies to all sizes.

Join with slip stitch as indicated unless otherwise stated.

Chain-2 at beginning of row counts as first half double crochet unless otherwise stated.

Special Stitch

Half double crochet join (hdc join): Place slip knot on hook, yo, insert hook in indicated st, yo and pull up a lp, yo, and draw through all lps on hook.

Slippers

Left Slipper

Leg

Row 1: With blue, ch 21 [25, 29], hdc in 3rd ch from hook *(beg sk chs count as first hdc)* and in each ch across, turn. *(20 [24, 28] hdc)*

Rows 2–14: Ch 2 *(see Pattern Notes)*, hdc in each hdc across, turn.

Top of Foot

Row 1: Ch 2, hdc in next 9 [11, 13] hdc, leaving rem sts unworked, turn. *(10 [12, 14] hdc)*

Rows 2–10: Ch 2, hdc in each hdc across, turn.

Row 11: Ch 2, **hdc dec** *(see Stitch Guide)* in next 2 hdc, hdc in each of next 4 [6, 8] sts, hdc dec in next 2 hdc, hdc in last hdc, turn. *(8 [10, 12] hdc)*

Row 12: Ch 2, hdc dec in next 2 hdc, hdc in each of next 2 [4, 6] hdc, hdc dec in next 2 sts, hdc in last hdc, turn. Fasten off size small only. *(6 [8, 10] hdc)*

Sizes Medium & Large Only

Row [13]: Ch 2, hdc dec in next 2 hdc, hdc in each of next [2, 4] hdc, hdc dec in next 2 hdc, hdc in last hdc, turn. Fasten off size medium only. *([6, 8] hdc)*

Size Large Only

Row [14]: Ch 2, hdc dec in next 2 hdc, hdc in each of next 2 hdc, hdc dec in next 2 hdc, hdc in last hdc. Fasten off. *([6] hdc)*

Right Slipper

Leg

Rows 1–14: Rep rows 1–14 of Leg of Left Slipper. Fasten off.

Top of Foot

Row 1: Sk first 10 [12, 14] hdc, **hdc join** *(see Special Stitch)* in next st, hdc in rem sts, turn. *(10 [12, 14] hdc)*

Rows 2–12 [2–13, 2–14]: Rep rows 2–12 [2–13, 2–14] of Top of Foot of Left Slipper.

Sole
Make 2.

Row 1: With taupe, ch 7, sc in 2nd ch from hook and in each ch across, turn. *(6 sc)*

Row 2: Ch 1, sc in first sc, 2 sc in next sc, sc in each sc across to last 2 sc, 2 sc in next sc, sc in last sc, turn. *(8 sc)*

Row 3: Ch 1, sc in each sc across, turn.

Rows 4 & 5 [4–7, 4–9]: Rep rows 2 and 3 once [twice, 3 times]. *(10 [12, 14] sc)*

Rows 6–20 [8–22, 10–24]: Ch 1, sc in first sc and in each sc across, turn.

Row 21 [23, 25]: Ch 1, sc in first sc, **sc dec** *(see Stitch Guide)* in next 2 sc, sc in each sc across to last 3 sc, sc dec in next 2 sc, sc in last sc, turn. *(8 [10, 12] sc)*

Row 22 [24, 26]: Ch 1 sc in first sc and in each sc across, turn.

Size Small Only
Rows 23 & 24: Rep rows 21 and 22. Fasten off. *(6 sc)*

Size Medium Only
Rows [25–28]: Rep rows 23 and 24. Fasten off. *([6] sc)*

Size Large Only
Rows [27–32]: [Rep rows 25 and 26] 3 times. Fasten off. *([6] sc)*

Assembly
Fold Leg in half with RS tog, matching ends of rows, sew tog last 2 rows at base of Leg.

Match RS of Sole and RS of Top of Foot and Leg opening and pin in place. With blue, loosely sl st Sole to Slipper, join in beg sl st and fasten off. Turn RS out.

Join blue at bottom of side opening of Slipper, sc evenly along ends of rows, across opposite side of foundation ch and along ends of rows on other side of opening. Fasten off.

Rep for 2nd Slipper.

Finishing
Ties
Make 2.

With taupe, beg with 5-inch tail, ch 80, fasten off, leaving 5-inch tail.

Using photo as a guide, lace Ties through side openings of Slippers.

Pompom
Make 4.

With taupe, make small (approximately 1½-inch) pompom. Using 5-inch tail, attach 1 pompom to each end of ch. ●

Rock Ridge Shawl

Design by Kathleen Berlew

Skill Level
■■□□ EASY

Finished Measurements
13 inches wide x 60 inches long, excluding Fringe

Materials
- Cascade Yarns 220 Superwash light/medium (DK/worsted) weight superwash wool yarn (3½ oz/220 yds/100g per ball):
    2 balls each #874 ridge rock and #1910 summer sky heather
    1 ball each #811 Como blue and #816 grey
- Size I/9/5.5mm crochet hook or size needed to obtain gauge
- Tapestry needle

3 LIGHT / **4** MEDIUM

Gauge

15 dc = 4 inches; 9 rows = 4 inches

Pattern Notes

Weave in loose ends as work progresses.

Chain-3 at beginning of row counts as first double crochet unless otherwise stated.

Beginning with row 2, refer to Color Sequences for correct color of each row. Work color changes as needed at end of each row.

Join with slip stitch as indicated unless otherwise stated.

Special Stitches

Shell: 3 dc in indicated st.

Popcorn (pc): 5 dc in indicated st, drop lp from hook, insert hook from front to back in top of first dc, pick up dropped lp, draw through st on hook.

Color Sequences

Rows 1, 2, 7, 15, 23, 27, 32, 33: Ridge rock.

Rows 3, 4, 13, 14, 19, 20, 28, 29: Grey.

Rows 5, 6, 11, 12, 21, 22, 30, 31: Como blue.

Rows 8, 9, 10, 16, 17, 18, 24, 25, 26: Summer sky heather.

Shawl

Row 1 (RS): With ridge rock, ch 227, dc in 4th ch from hook *(beg sk chs count as first dc)* and in each ch across, turn. *(225 dc)*

Row 2: Ch 3 *(see Pattern Notes)*, dc in next st, [ch 1, sk next st, dc in next st] 111 times, dc in top of beg ch-3, **change color** *(see Stitch Guide)* in last dc as needed to color indicated in **Color Sequences** *(see Pattern Notes)*, turn. *(114 dc, 111 ch-1 sps)*

Row 3: Ch 3, dc in each dc and ch-1 sp across, ending with dc in top of beg ch-3, turn. *(225 dc)*

Row 4: Ch 3, dc in next dc, sk 1 dc, **shell** *(see Special Stitches)* in next dc, [sk 2 dc, shell in next dc] 73 times, sk 1 dc, dc in top of beg ch-3, turn. *(74 shells, 3 dc)*

Row 5: Ch 3, [dc in first 2 dc of next shell, dc in sp between current shell and next shell] 73 times, dc in first 2 dc of next shell, dc in sp between current shell and next dc, dc in next dc, dc in top of beg ch-3, turn. *(225 dc)*

Rows 6 & 7: Rep rows 2 and 3.

Row 8: Rep row 2.

Row 9: Ch 3, [**pc** *(see Special Stitches)* in next dc, dc in next ch-1 sp, dc in next dc, dc in next ch-1 sp] 55 times, pc in next dc, dc in next ch-1 sp, dc in next dc, dc in top of beg ch-3, turn. *(56 pc, 169 dc)*

Rows 10–13: [Rep rows 2 and 3] twice.

Rows 14 & 15: Rep rows 4 and 5.

Row 16: Rep row 2.

Row 17: Rep row 9.

Rows 18–25: Rep rows 10–17.

Rows 26–32: Rep rows 10–16.

Row 33: Rep row 3. Fasten off.

Fringe
Row 1: With RS of short edge facing, **join** (see Pattern Notes) ridge rock to end of first row, working in ends of rows, ch 1, 2 sc in same row and in each row across, turn. (66 sc)

Row 2: [Ch 30, sl st in next 2 sc] 32 times, ch 30, sl st in last sc. Fasten off. (33 ch-30 lps)

Rep rows 1 and 2 on rem short edge of Shawl.

Block to finished measurements.

Boho Beaded Key Chain

Design by Debra Arch

Skill Level
 INTERMEDIATE

Finished Measurements
1¼ inches wide x 4½ inches long, excluding fringe

Materials
- Caron Little Crafties medium (worsted) weight acrylic yarn (¾ oz/63 yds/20g per skein): ½ skein of desired color for each key chain

- Size F/5/3.75mm crochet hook or size needed to obtain gauge
- Size J/10/6mm crochet hook for tassel assembly (optional)
- 10–15mm beads in desired colors, 3 for each key chain
- 1¼-inch-diameter metal key ring, 1 for each key chain
- Beading needle or dental floss threader
- Stitch marker
- 4-inch square cardboard
- Tapestry needle

Gauge
2 sc rows = ½ inch; 5 sc = 1¼ inches

Pattern Note
Chain-1 at beginning of round does not count as a stitch.

Special Stitches

Partial front post treble crochet (partial fptr): Yo twice, insert hook around post of indicated st, yo, pull up lp, [yo, pull through 2 lps on hook] twice *(2 lps rem on hook)*, insert hook in last sc, yo, pull up lp, yo, pull through all 3 lps on hook. This st counts as a fptr in st counts.

Front post treble crochet 2 together (fptr2tog): Yo twice, insert hook around post of first indicated st from front to back to front again, yo, pull up lp, [yo, pull through 2 lps on hook] twice *(2 lps rem on hook)*, yo twice, insert hook around post of next indicated st from front to back to front again, yo, pull up lp, [yo, pull through 2 lps on hook] twice, yo, pull through rem 3 lps on hook.

Slide bead (sb): Slide bead up close to hook.

Boho Beaded Key Chain

Thread 3 beads onto yarn using beading needle or dental floss threader, leaving a 9-inch beg yarn tail, make a slip knot and place on hook.

Row 1 (RS): Beg at top of key chain, ch 6, sc in 2nd ch from hook and in each ch across, turn. *(5 sc)*

Row 2: Ch 1 *(see Pattern Note)*, sc in first st and in each st across, turn.

Row 3: Rep row 2. Place st marker around post of 3rd (center) st.

Row 4: Rep row 2.

Row 5: Ch 1, **fptr** *(see Stitch Guide)* around post of marked st 2 rows below, sc in each of next 3 sts, **partial fptr** *(see Special Stitches)* around post of same marked st *(diamond tip made)*, turn. *(3 sc, 2 fptr)*

Row 6: Rep row 2.

Row 7: Ch 1, fptr around post of first fptr 2 rows below, sc in next st, **sb** *(see Special Stitches)*, tightly, ch 1, pushing bead to RS, sk next st, sc in next st, partial fptr around post of next fptr 2 rows below, turn. *(2 sc, 2 fptr, 1 ch-1 bead sp)*

Row 8: Ch 1, sc in first st, sc in next st, sc in next ch-1 sp, sc in each of next 2 sts, turn. *(5 sc)*

Row 9: Ch 1, sc in first st, sc in next st, **fptr2tog** *(see Special Stitches)* around posts of fptr 2 rows below *(diamond tip made)*, sc in each of next 2 sts, turn. *(4 sc, fptr2tog)*

Row 10: Rep row 2.

Row 11: Ch 1, fptr around post of fptr2tog *(diamond tip)* 2 rows below, sc in each of next 3 sts, partial fptr around post of same fptr2tog, turn. *(3 sc, 2 fptr)*

Rows 12–17: Rep rows 6–11.

Note: To create longer key chains, rep last 6 rows to desired length, ending with a rep of row 9, then work row 22 for tassel opening. A longer key chain will require more beads.

Rows 18–21: Rep rows 6–9.

Row 22: Ch 1, **sc dec** *(see Stitch Guide)* in first 2 sts, ch 1, sk next st *(tassel opening made)*, sc dec in next 2 sts. Fasten off. *(2 sc)*

Finishing

Fold rows 1 and 2 of key chain through center of key ring and use beg yarn tail and tapestry needle to whipstitch opposite side of foundation chain to WS of key chain.

Tassels

Wrap 1 strand of desired yarn color 15 times around 4-inch cardboard. Use scissors to cut yarn along bottom edge of cardboard. Use size J crochet hook to pull yarn strands halfway through ch-1 sp of row 22 of key chain. Smooth tassel and fold in half over bottom edge of key chain with yarn ends even. Cut a 24-inch length of yarn, fold in half and wrap doubled strand several times around tassel ends approximately ⅜-inch below fold. Knot ends tightly on WS to secure. Thread tie ends through tapestry needle, insert needle from top to bottom under wraps and through center of tassel to hide ends. Use scissors to trim tassel ends evenly to desired length. ●

Snowcapped Beanie

Design by Bendy Carter

Skill Level

 ■□□ EASY

Finished Measurements

Height: 8¼ inches

Circumference: 21½ inches

Materials

- Tahki Yarns Scotland light (DK) weight merino wool yarn (1¾ oz/ 174 yds/50g per ball):
    - 1 ball each #01 cream and #08 denim
- Size H/8/5mm crochet hook or size needed to obtain gauge
- Stitch markers
- 2½-inch pompom maker or cardboard circles
- Tapestry needle

Gauge

15 sts = 4 inches; 21 sc rows = 4 inches

Pattern Notes

Weave in loose ends as work progresses.

Mark first stitch of round; move marker up with each round.

Work in continuous rounds; do not turn or join unless otherwise stated.

When working a 2-color round, place color not being used on wrong side of fabric and crochet over it.

Chain-2 at beginning of round counts as first half double crochet unless otherwise stated.

Join with slip stitch unless otherwise stated.

Special Stitches

Split single crochet (split sc): Insert hook between legs of next st *(see illustration)*, yo, draw through st, yo, draw through both lps on hook.

Split Single Crochet

Split single crochet decrease (split sc dec): [Insert hook between legs of next st, yo, draw through st] twice, yo, draw through all 3 lps on hook.

Cap

Rnd 1 (RS): With denim, ch 80, being careful not to twist ch, sc in beg ch to form ring, **place marker** *(see Pattern Notes)* in st just made, sc in each ch around, **do not join** *(see Pattern Notes)*. (80 sts)

Rnd 2: [Crocheting **over cream** *(see Pattern Notes)* **split sc** *(see Special Stitches)* in each of next 7 sts changing to cream in last st, split sc in next st changing to denim] 10 times. *(10 cream sts, 70 denim sts)*

Rnd 3: Drop cream to back of work, split sc in each st around.

Rnd 4: [Crocheting over cream split sc in each of next 3 sts changing to cream in last st, split sc in next st changing to denim, crocheting over cream split sc in each of next 4 sts] 10 times.

Rnd 5: Rep rnd 3.

Rnds 6 & 7: Rep rnds 2 and 3.

Rnd 8: [Crocheting over cream split sc in next st changing to cream, split sc in next st changing to denim, crocheting over cream split sc in each of next 2 sts] 20 times.

Rnd 9: Rep rnd 3.

Rnd 10: [Crocheting over cream split sc in each of next 3 sts changing to cream in last st, split sc in next st changing to denim] 20 times.

Rnd 11: Rep rnd 8.

Rnd 12: [Crocheting over cream split sc in each of next 3 sts changing to cream in last st, split sc in next st changing to denim] 19 times, crocheting over cream split sc in each of next 3 sts changing to cream in last st, split sc in next st.

Rnd 13: [Split sc in next st changing to denim, split sc in next st changing to cream] 39 times, split sc in next st changing to denim, split sc in next st.

Rnd 14: [Split sc in next st changing to cream, split sc in next st changing to denim] 39 times, split sc in next st changing to cream, split sc in next st.

Rnd 15: [Crocheting over denim split sc in each of next 3 sts changing to denim in last st, split sc in next st changing to cream] 20 times.

Rnd 16: [Crocheting over denim split sc in next st changing to denim, split sc in next st changing to

cream, crocheting over denim split sc in each of next 2 sts] 20 times.

Rnd 17: Rep rnd 15.

Rnd 18: Drop denim to back of work, split sc in each st around.

Rnd 19: Rep rnd 16.

Rnd 20: Rep rnd 18.

Cap Shaping

Rnd 1: [With cream, crocheting over denim split sc in each of next 2 sts, **split sc dec** *(see Special Stitches)* in next 2 sts, split sc in each of next 3 sts changing to denim in last st, split sc in next st changing to cream] 10 times. *(70 sts)*

Rnd 2: Drop denim to back of work, split sc in each st around.

Rnd 3: Crocheting over denim split sc in each of first 2 sts changing to denim in last st, split sc in next st changing to cream, [crocheting over denim split sc in each of next 2 sts, split sc dec in next 2 sts, split sc in each of next 2 sts changing to denim in last st, split sc in next st changing to cream] 9 times, crocheting over denim split sc in each of next 2 sts, split sc dec in last 2 sts. *(60 sts)*

Rnd 4: Rep rnd 2.

Rnd 5: Crocheting over denim split sc dec in first 2 sts, split sc in each of next 3 sts, split sc dec in next 2 sts, split sc in each of next 3 sts changing to denim in last st, [split sc in next st changing to cream, crocheting over denim split sc dec in next 2 sts, split sc in each of next 4 sts, split sc dec in next 2 sts, split sc in each of next 3 sts changing to denim in last st] 4 times, split sc in next st changing to cream, split sc in last st. *(50 sts)*

Rnd 6: Rep rnd 2.

Rnd 7: Crocheting over denim split sc in each of first 3 sts changing to denim in last st, [split sc in next st changing to cream, crocheting over denim split sc dec in next 2 sts, split sc in each of next 3 sts, split sc dec in next 2 sts, split sc in each of next 2 sts changing to denim in last st] 4 times, split sc in next st changing to cream, crocheting over denim split sc dec in next 2 sts, split sc in each of next 2 sts, split sc dec in last 2 sts. Fasten off denim. *(40 sts)*

Rnd 8: With cream split sc in each st around.

Rnd 9: [Split sc in each of next 2 sts, split sc dec in next 2 sts] 10 times. *(30 sts)*

Rnd 10: Rep rnd 8.

Rnd 11: [Split sc in each of next 4 sts, split sc dec in next 2 sts] 5 times. *(25 sts)*

Rnd 12: [Split sc in each of next 3 sts, split sc dec in next 2 sts] 5 times. *(20 sts)*

Rnd 13: [Split sc in each of next 2 sts, split sc dec in next 2 sts] 5 times. *(15 sts)*

Rnd 14: [Split sc in next st, split sc dec in next 2 sts] 5 times. *(10 sts)*

Rnd 15: [Split sc dec in next 2 sts] 5 times. Fasten off cream leaving long end for sewing. *(5 sts)*

Weave end through sts on last rnd, pull tight to close.

Brim

Rnd 1 (RS): Join *(see Pattern Notes)* denim in unused lp of beg ch on Cap, **ch 2** *(see Pattern Notes)*, [crocheting sts around post of sts on rnd 1 of Cap, **fpdc** *(see Stitch Guide)* around post of next st, **bpdc** *(see Special Stitches)* around post of next st] 39 times, fpdc around post of last st, join in top of beg ch-2. *(80 sts)*

Rnd 2: Ch 2, [fpdc around post of next st, bpdc around post of next st] 39 times, fpdc around post of last st, join in top of beg ch-2.

Rnds 3–5: [Rep rnd 2] 3 times. Fasten off at end of last rnd.

Pompom

Use pompom maker, or cut 2 cardboard circles with 2½-inch diameter. Cut a hole in the center of each circle, about ½ inch in diameter. Thread a tapestry needle with a length of yarn doubled. Holding both circles tog, insert needle through center hole, over the outside edge, and through center again *(see Fig. 1 of illustration below)* until entire circle is covered and center hole is filled (thread more length of yarn as needed).

With sharp scissors, cut yarn between the 2 circles all around the circumference *(see Fig. 2).*

Using 2 12-inch strands of yarn, slip yarn between circles and overlap yarn ends 2 or 3 times to prevent knot from slipping *(see Fig. 3)*, pull tightly and tie into a firm knot.

Remove cardboard and fluff out Pompom by rolling it between your hands. Trim even with scissors; leave the tying ends for when attaching Pompom to project. ●

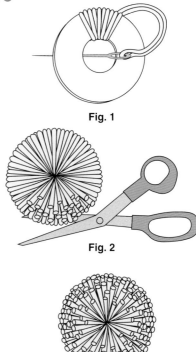

Fig. 1

Fig. 2

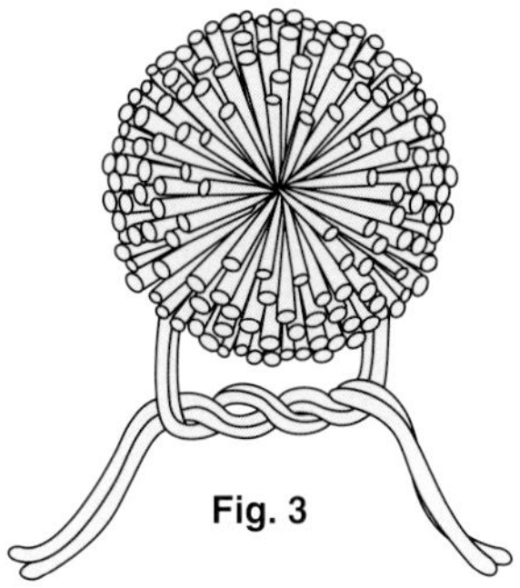

Fig. 3

Mega Baskets

Designs by Debra Arch

Skill Level

 EASY

Finished Sizes

Instructions written for small basket; color changes for medium and large baskets are given in [ ].

Finished Measurements

Small Basket: 8 inches in diameter x 7 inches high

Medium Basket: 10 inches in diameter x 7 inches high

Large Basket: 12 inches in diameter x 7 inches high

Materials

- Plymouth Yarn Encore Mega super bulky (super chunky) weight acrylic/wool yarn (3½ oz/64 yds/ 100g per skein):
    - 2 skeins each #146 cream (C1), #577 bison (C5) and #692 citron (C4)
    - 3 skeins each #199 aqua (C3) and #658 bluebell (MC)
    - 4 skeins #379 ash grey (C2)
- Size H/8/5mm crochet hook or size needed to obtain gauge
- Tapestry needle

Gauge

Rnds 1–3 = 3¾ inches in diameter

Pattern Notes

Weave in loose ends as work progresses.

Join with slip stitch as indicated unless otherwise stated.

To change color, insert hook in indicated last stitch of round, yarn over with new color, pull up loop, yarn over, pull through both loops on hook. Fasten off old color.

Chain-3 at beginning of round counts as first double crochet unless otherwise stated.

Chain-1 at beginning of round does not count as a single crochet.

Special Stitch

Center single crochet (csc): Insert hook through inverted V-shape in center of indicated st, yo, pull up lp, yo, pull through both lps on hook.

Basket

Base

Rnd 1: (RS): With MC [C2, C5], make a **slip ring** (see illustration), **ch 3** (see Pattern Notes), 11 dc in ring, **join** (see Pattern Notes) in 3rd ch of beg ch-3. Draw beg length of yarn tightly to close opening. (12 dc)

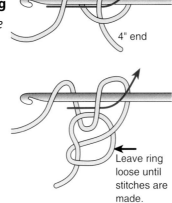

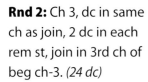

Slip Ring

4" end

Leave ring loose until stitches are made.

Rnd 2: Ch 3, dc in same ch as join, 2 dc in each rem st, join in 3rd ch of beg ch-3. (24 dc)

Rnd 3: Ch 3, dc in same ch as join, dc in next st, [2 dc in next st, dc in next st] around, join in 3rd ch of beg ch-3. (36 dc)

Rnd 4: Ch 3, dc in same ch as join, dc in each of next 2 sts, [2 dc in next st, dc in each of next 2 sts] around, join in 3rd ch of beg ch-3. (48 dc)

Rnd 5: Rep rnd 4. (64 dc)

Rnd 6: Ch 3, dc in same ch as join, dc in each of next 3 sts, [2 dc in next st, dc in each of next 3 sts] around, join in 3rd ch of beg ch-3. (80 dc)

Small Basket

Rnd 7: Ch 1, sc in same ch as join, sc in each of next 9 sts, [2 sc in next st, sc in each of next 9 sts] around, join in beg sc. (88 sc)

Rnd 8: Ch 1, working in **back lps** (see Stitch Guide), sc in first st and in each st around, join in beg sc.

Rnd 9: Ch 1, **csc** (see Special Stitch) in first st, sc in back lp of next st, [csc in next st, sc in back lp of next st] around, join in beg sc. (88 sts)

Rnds 10 & 11: Rep rnd 9, **changing color** (see Pattern Notes) to C1 in joining sl st at end of rnd 11.

Rnds 12 & 13: Rep rnd 9, changing color to C2 in joining sl st at end of rnd 13.

Rnds 14–16: Rep rnd 9, changing color to C3 in joining sl st at end of rnd 16.

Rnd 17: Rep rnd 9.

Rnd 18: Rep rnd 9, changing color to C4 at end of rnd.

Rnds 19 & 20: Rep rnds 10 and 11, changing color to C1 in joining sl st at end of rnd 20.

Rnd 21: Rep rnd 9, changing color to C3 at end of rnd.

Rnd 22: Rep rnd 9, changing color to C2 at end of rnd.

Rnds 23–25: Rep rnd 9, changing color to C1 at end of rnd 25.

Rnds 26 & 27: Rep rnd 9, changing color to MC at end of rnd 27.

Rnds 28–32: Rep rnd 9. Fasten off at end of last rnd.

Medium Basket

Rnd 7: Ch 3, dc in same ch as join, dc in each of next 9 sts, [2 dc in next st, dc in each of next 9 sts] around, join in beg sc. (88 dc)

Rnd 8: Ch 1, sc in first st and in each of next 4 sts, [2 sc in next st, sc in each of next 10 sts] around to last 6 sts, 2 sc in next st, sc in each of next 5 sts, join in beg sc. (96 sc)

Rnd 9: Rep rnd 8 of Small Basket, **changing color** (see Pattern Notes) to C5 in last sc.

Rnd 10 and all even rnds: Ch 1, **csc** (see Special Stitch) in first st, sc in back lp of next st, [csc in next st, sc in back lp of next st] around, join in beg sc, change color to C2.

Rnd 11: Rep rnd 10, changing color to C3 at end of rnd.

Rnd 13: Rep rnd 10, changing color to C1 at end of rnd.

Rnd 15: Rep rnd 10, changing color to C4 at end of rnd.

Rnd 17: Rep rnd 10, changing color to MC at end of rnd.

Rnd 19: Rep rnd 10, changing color to C5 at end of rnd.

Rnd 21: Rep rnd 10, changing color to MC at end of rnd.

Rnd 23: Rep rnd 10, changing color to C4 at end of rnd.

Rnd 25: Rep rnd 10, changing color to C1 at end of rnd.

Rnd 27: Rep rnd 10, changing color to C3 at end of rnd.

Rnd 29: Rep rnd 10, changing color to C5 at end of rnd.

Rnd 31: Rep rnd 10. At end of rnd, do not change color. Fasten off.

Large Basket

Rnd 7: Rep rnd 7 of Medium Basket.

Rnd 8: Ch 3, dc in first st and in each of next 4 sts, [2 dc in next st, dc in each of next 10 sts] around, 2 dc in next st, dc in each of next 5 sts, join in 3rd ch of beg ch-3. *(96 dc)*

Rnd 9: Ch 3, dc in first st and in each of next 11 sts, [2 dc in next st, dc in each of next 11 sts] around, join in 3rd ch of beg ch-3. *(104 dc)*

Rnd 10: Ch 3, dc in first st and in each of next 7 sts, [2 dc in next st, dc in each of next 7 sts] around, join in 3rd ch of beg ch-3. *(116 dc)*

Rnd 11: Rep rnd 8 of Small Basket, **changing color** *(see Pattern Notes)* to C3 in joining sl st at end of rnd.

Rnd 12: Ch 1, **csc** *(see Special Stitch)* in first st, sc in back lp of next st, [csc in next st, sc in back lp of next st] around, join in beg sc.

Rnds 13–16: Rep rnd 12, changing color to C1 at end of rnd 16.

Rnd 17: Rep rnd 12, changing color to C4 at end of rnd.

Rnds 18–23: Rep rnds 12–17, changing color to MC at end of rnd 23.

Rnds 24–29: Rep rnds 12–17, changing color to C2 at end of rnd 29.

Rnds 30–34: Rep rnd 12. At end of last rnd, fasten off. ●

Aran Honeycomb Scarf

Design by Bonnie Barker

Skill Level

 ■ ■ ■ ▢ INTERMEDIATE

Finished Measurements

7½ inches wide x 55 inches long

Materials

- Berroco Ultra Alpaca Light light (DK) weight alpaca/wool yarn (1¾ oz/144 yds/50g per hank):
  5 hanks #42188 lunar mix
- Size H/8/5mm crochet hook or size needed to obtain gauge
- Tapestry needle

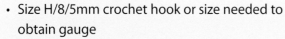 **3** LIGHT

Gauge

In honeycomb st (rows 9–12): 23 sts = 4 inches; 11 rows = 4 inches

Pattern Notes

Weave in loose ends as work progresses.

Chain-2 at beginning of row counts as first half double crochet unless otherwise stated.

Scarf

Ch 40.

Row 1: Dc in 4th ch from hook *(beg sk chs count as first dc)* and in each ch across. *(38 dc)*

Row 2: Ch 2 *(see Pattern Notes)*, sk first st, [**fpdc** *(see Stitch Guide)* around next 2 sts, **bpdc** *(see Stitch Guide)* around next 2 sts] across, hdc in turning ch, turn.

Rows 3–8: Rep row 2.

Row 9: Ch 2, bpdc around next 2 sts, fpdc around next 2 sts, bpdc around next 2 sts, [sk next 2 sts, fpdc

around next 2 sts, working behind last 2 sts, fpdc around 2 sk sts, sk next 2 sts, fpdc around next 2 sts, working in front of last 2 sts, fpdc around 2 sk sts] 3 times, fpdc around next 2 sts, bpdc around next 2 sts, fpdc around next 2 sts, hdc in turning ch, turn.

Row 10: Ch 2, bpdc around next 2 sts, fpdc around next 2 sts, bpdc around next 26 sts, fpdc around next 2 sts, bpdc around next 2 sts, fpdc around next 2 sts, hdc in turning ch, turn.

Row 11: Ch 2, fpdc around next 2 sts, bpdc around next 2 sts, fpdc around next 2 sts, [sk next 2 sts, fpdc around next 2 sts, working in front of last 2 sts, fpdc around 2 sk sts, sk next 2 sts, fpdc around next 2 sts, working behind last 2 sts, fpdc around 2 sk sts] 3 times, bpdc around next 2 sts, fpdc in next 2 sts, bpdc around next 2 sts, hdc in turning ch, turn.

Row 12: Ch 2, fpdc around next 2 sts, bpdc around next 2 sts, fpdc around next 2 sts, bpdc around next

24 sts, bpdc around next 2 sts, fpdc around next 2 sts, bpdc around next 2 sts, hdc in turning ch, turn.

Rows 13–152: [Rep rows 9–12] 35 times or to desired length, ending last rep on row 12.

Rows 153–160: Ch 2, [bpdc around next 2 sts, fpdc around next 2 sts] across, hdc in turning ch, turn. Fasten off at the end of row 160. ●

For additional instructions, watch these helpful videos by designer Bonnie Barker:

Right-Hand Version: https://youtu.be/4dBf8yxy-OM

Left-Hand Version: https://youtu.be/dlTcuzFZfLI

Cat Kitchen Boa

Design by My Fingers Fly

Skill Level

 EASY

Finished Measurements

4 inches wide x 62 inches long

Materials

- Berroco Summer Sesame medium (worsted) weight cotton/acrylic/ nylon yarn (3½ oz/295 yds/ 100g per ball):
    1 ball #5235 marigold
- Medium (worsted) weight cotton yarn:
    20 yds white
    4 yds each black, peach and light blue
- Size G/6/4mm crochet hook or size needed to obtain gauge
- Stitch marker
- Tapestry needle
- Kitchen towel: approximately 16 inches wide x 25 inches long
- Sewing needle
- Sewing thread to match towel

Gauge

23 sc = 4 inches; 5 rows = 1 inch

Take time to check gauge.

Pattern Notes

Designer used Berroco Pima 100 yarn in #8400 yarrow, #8420 sea holly, #8434 black eyed Susan and #8429 zinnea for the cat's features.

Weave in loose ends as work progresses.

Join with slip stitch as indicated unless otherwise stated.

Cat head is worked first, then boa section. Second cat head is worked separately, then sewn to end of boa. Kitchen towel is cut in half widthwise and edges are finished with zigzag stitch by hand or on a sewing machine. Halves of the towel are then folded and sewn to the back of each cat head.

Kitchen Boa

Cat Head

Eye
Make 2.

With light blue, ch 2, 7 sc in 2nd ch from hook, **join** *(see Pattern Notes)* in first sc. Fasten off, leaving 4-inch length for sewing. Use black to embroider pupils on each eye.

Eye Patch
Rnd 1: With white, ch 2, 7 sc in 2nd ch from hook, join in first sc. *(7 sc)*

Rnd 2: Ch 1, 2 sc in each st around, join in first sc. *(14 sc)*

Rnd 3: Ch 1, sc in first st, 2 sc in next st, [sc in next st, 2 sc in next st] 6 times, join in first sc. Fasten off, leaving 6-inch length for sewing. *(21 sc)*

Head
Rnd 1: With marigold, ch 2, 12 sc in 2nd ch from hook. *(12 sc)*

Note: *Do not join. Work in continuous rnds unless otherwise specified. Mark first st with st marker and move up as work progresses.*

Rnd 2: [Sc in next st, 2 sc in next st] 6 times. *(18 sc)*

Rnd 3: [Sc in next 2 sts, 2 sc in next st] 6 times. *(24 sc)*

Rnd 4: [Sc in next 3 sts, 2 sc in next st] 6 times. *(30 sc)*

Rnd 5: Sc in each st around.

Rnd 6: [Sc in next 4 sts, 2 sc in next st] 6 times. *(36 sc)*

Rnd 7: Sc in each st around.

Rnd 8: [Sc in next 5 sts, 2 sc in next st] 6 times. *(42 sc)*

Rnd 9: Sc in each st around.

Rnd 10: [Sc in next 6 sts, 2 sc in next st] 6 times. *(48 sc)*

Rnd 11: Sc in each st around.

Rnd 12: [Sc in next 7 sts, 2 sc in next st] 6 times. *(54 sc)*

Rnds 13–23: Sc in each st around.

Rnd 24: Sc in each st around, join in first st to end spiral. Do not fasten off; remove hook from lp, insert st marker into lp to place lp on hold.

Face
Press sides of head flat with lp on hold at right-hand edge to define front and back of head. Sew eye patch to front of face over rnds 12–19. Sew one eye to eye patch and one eye to face over rnds 13–16; pupils should be oriented vertically.

Using peach, embroider a nose centered between the eyes and over rnds 4–6 using **straight stitch** *(see illustration)*.

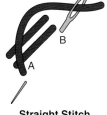

Straight Stitch

Top of Head
Row 25: Return to rnd 24 and pick up yarn, sc through both front and back at the same time to close opening. Do not fasten off. *(27 sc)*

Boa

Row 1: Turn, sl st in first 3 sts of Top of Head, ch 1, sc in same st as last sl st, sc in next 22 sts, turn, leaving rem 2 sts unworked. *(23 sc)*

Row 2: Ch 1, sc in each st across, turn.

Rep row 2 until piece measures approximately 32 inches from the top of the head. When finished and including the 2 halves of a 30-inch towel, kitchen boa will measure approximately 62 inches. If a longer or shorter boa is desired, adjust the number of rows here.

2nd Head

Rep Cat Head through end of Face, sewing eye patch under opposite eye.

Rep Top of Head and fasten off. Sew center 23 sts of row 25 to the opposite end of the Boa.

Ear

Make 4.

Row 1: With white, ch 4, sc in 2nd ch from hook, sc in each of last 2 chs, turn. *(3 sc)*

Row 2: Ch 1, sc in each st across, turn.

Row 3: Ch 1, **sc dec** *(see Stitch Guide)* in first 2 sts, sc in last st, turn. *(2 sc)*

Row 4: Ch 1, sc in each st across, turn.

Row 5: Ch 1, sc dec in rem 2 sts. Fasten off. *(1 sc)*

Border

Join marigold to first row end at bottom corner of ear, sc in each row end, 2 sc in sc of row 5, rotate to work across next side, sc in each row end, work an additional sc in last row end, rotate to work across unused lps of foundation ch, sc in each of first 2 chs, 2 sc in last ch, join in first sc. *(17 sc)*

Fasten off, leaving 6-inch length for sewing. Sew 2 ears to top of each Head with outer edge of each Ear even with outer edge of Head.

Assembly

Cut towel in half widthwise and serge or zigzag raw top edges. Fold side *(uncut)* edges of each half to meet in the middle and sew top *(cut)* edge to secure folds.

Fold side edges again to meet in the middle and sew top edge. This will give a width of approximately 4 inches.

Hand- or machine-sew cut edge of towel to back side of each cat head, centering the towel with the cat head.

If ears are curling, block to straighten. ●

Reversible Checkerboard Cowl

Design by Mary Forte

Skill Level

 INTERMEDIATE

Finished Measurements

Circumference: 22 inches

Height: 7½ inches

Materials

- Premier Basix Chunky bulky (chunky) weight acrylic yarn (3½ oz/117 yds/100g per skein):
    1 skein #1145-03 linen (MC)
- Premier Colorfusion Chunky bulky (chunky) weight acrylic yarn (3½ oz/109 yds/100g per skein):
    1 skein #1174-04 neapolitan (CC)
- Size N/13/9mm crochet hook or size needed to obtain gauge
- Locking stitch marker
- Tapestry needle

Gauge

10 dc = 4 inches; 6 dc pattern rows = 4 inches

To save time, take time to check gauge.

Pattern Notes

This cowl begins with foundation double crochet. Then each round is worked twice—once with each color—up to the top border. The border rounds are worked only once.

Join with a slip stitch unless otherwise stated.

Chain-1 at the beginning of a round does not count as a stitch.

Chain-3 at the beginning of a round counts as the first double crochet of the round. On following rounds, work into the 3rd chain of the chain-3 as for a double crochet.

When working the 2nd half of a double round, you can fold the first half back to get it out of the way.

When working into the skipped stitches of the previous round, insert hook into the double crochet and under the chain-2. Complete the double crochet normally.

When there is a slip stitch at the top of a double crochet or chain, ignore it and work into the double crochet or chain.

When changing colors, be sure to keep the old yarn to the front and out of the way of the new stitches.

When marking a stitch, pull the loop out 1–2 inches to make it easier to find. Tighten it back up when you put it back on the hook.

Special Stitches

First foundation double crochet (first foundation dc): Ch 2, yo, insert hook in 2nd ch from hook *(see illustration A)*, yo, pull up lp, yo, draw through 1 lp on hook *(see illustration B—ch-1 completed)*, [yo, draw through 2 lps on hook] twice *(see illustrations C–E—dc completed)*.

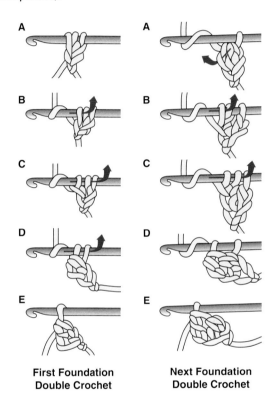

First Foundation Double Crochet

Next Foundation Double Crochet

Next foundation double crochet (next foundation dc): *Yo, insert hook in last ch-1 made *(see illustration A)*, yo, pull up lp, yo, draw through 1 lp on hook *(see illustration B—ch-1 completed)*, [yo, draw through 2 lps on hook] twice *(see illustrations C–E—dc completed)*, rep from * as indicated.

Cowl

Rnd 1: With MC, **first foundation dc** *(see Special Stitches)*, 51 **next foundation dc** *(see Special Stitches)*, taking care to not twist the row, **join** *(see Pattern Notes)* to first foundation dc, using tapestry needle,

wrap beg tail around last base ch to join. *(52 foundation dc)*

Rnd 2A: Continuing with MC, **ch 3** *(see Pattern Notes)*, dc in next dc, ch 2, sk next 2 dc, [dc in next 2 dc, ch 2, sk next 2 dc] to end of rnd, join at top of beg ch, sl st in next dc, remove hook, place locking marker in last lp, and leave MC and the lp in front of work. *(13 dc pairs and 13 ch-2 sps)*

Rnd 2B: *(See Pattern Notes)* Join CC and working in front of the sts from rnd 2A, sl st in first sk dc, ch 3, dc in next sk dc, ch 2, sk 2 dc, [dc in each of next 2 sk dc, ch 2, sk 2 dc] to end of rnd, making sure that MC and its lp are still at front, join in first st of rnd, sl st in next dc, switch positions of hook and marker, leaving CC and its lp at front of work. *(13 dc pairs and 13 ch sps)*

Rnd 3A: With MC, sl st into next sk dc, ch 3, dc into next sk dc, ch 2, sk next 2 dc, [dc in each of next 2 sk dc, ch 2, sk next 2 dc] to end of rnd, making sure CC and its lp are still at front, join in first st of rnd, sl st in next st, switch the positions of the hook and the marker, leaving last lp and MC in front of work.

Rnd 3B: Working with CC in front of the sts from rnd 3A, sl st into next sk dc, ch 3, dc into next sk dc, ch 2, sk 2 dc, [dc in each of next 2 sk dc, ch 2, sk 2 dc] to end of rnd, making sure MC and its lp are still at front, join in first st of rnd, sl st in next st, switch the positions of the hook and marker, leaving last lp and CC in front of work.

Rnds 4–9: [Rep both halves (A and B) of rnd 3] 6 more times, remove marker, fasten off CC.

Rnd 10: With MC, sl st into next sk dc, ch 3, dc into each sk dc to end of rnd, join in 3rd st of beg ch. *(52 dc)*

Rnd 11: Ch 1 *(see Pattern Notes)*, sc in same st as join, sc in each dc around, join in beg sc, fasten off. *(52 sc)*

Finishing

Weave in ends and block. ●

Double Six Tote

Design by Kathleen Berlew

Skill Level

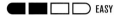 EASY

Finished Measurements

17 inches wide x 15 inches high

Materials

- Bernat Super Value medium (worsted) weight acrylic yarn (7 oz/426 yds/197g per skein):
    1 skein each #0608 bright yellow (A), #3046 soft gray (B), #0615 carrot (C), #3402 magenta (D) and #3042 dark gray (E)
- Size J/10/6mm crochet hook or size needed to obtain gauge
- Tapestry needle
- Stitch markers

Gauge

13 sts = 4 inches in shell/ch-1 pattern; 5 rnds = 4 inches

Pattern Notes

The design is worked with a double strand of worsted-weight yarn making it extra sturdy.

Tote is worked in two hexagonal panels that are joined.

Join with slip stitch unless otherwise stated.

Weave in ends as work progresses.

Start each new color join in a different corner of the hexagon.

Special Stitches

Beginning shell (beg shell): Ch 3, dc in indicated sp or st.

Shell: 2 dc in indicated sp or st.

Beginning corner shell (beg corner shell): (Ch 3, dc, ch 1, 2 dc) in indicated sp or st.

Corner shell: (2 dc, ch 1, 2 dc) in indicated sp or st.

Tote

Front/Back

Make 2.

Rnd 1 (RS): With **2 strands** (see Pattern Notes) of A held tog, make a **slip ring** (see illustration), **beg shell** (see Special Stitches) in ring, ch 1, [**shell** (see Special Stitches), ch 1] 5 times in ring, **join** (see Pattern Notes) in top of beg ch-3, pull ring to close. (6 shells)

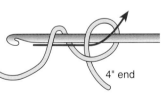

4" end

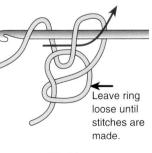

Leave ring loose until stitches are made.

Slip Ring

Rnd 2: Sl st in next dc and next ch-1 sp, **beg corner shell** *(see Special Stitches)* in same sp, ch 1, [**corner shell** *(see Special Stitches)*, ch 1] in each ch-1 sp around, join in top of beg ch-3. Fasten off. *(6 corner shells)*

Rnd 3: Join B in any corner ch-1 sp, beg corner shell in same sp, ch 1, shell in next ch-1 sp, ch 1, [corner shell in next corner ch-1 sp, ch 1, shell in next ch-1 sp, ch 1] around, join in top of beg ch-3. Fasten off. *(6 corner shells, 6 shells)*

Rnd 4: Join C in **any corner ch-1 sp** *(see Pattern Notes)*, beg corner shell in same sp, ch 1, [shell in next ch-1 sp, ch 1] twice, *corner shell in next corner ch-1 sp, ch 1, [shell in next ch-1 sp, ch 1] twice, rep from * around, join in top of beg ch-3. *(6 corner shells, 12 shells)*

Rnd 5: Sl st in next dc and ch-1 sp, beg corner shell in same sp, ch 1, [shell in next ch-1 sp, ch 1] 3 times, *corner shell in next corner ch-1 sp, ch 1, [shell in next ch-1 sp, ch 1] 3 times, rep from * around, join in top of beg ch-3. Fasten off. *(6 corner shells, 18 shells)*

Rnd 6: Join D in any corner ch sp, beg corner shell in same sp, ch 1, [shell in next ch-1 sp, ch 1] 4 times, *corner shell in next corner ch-1 sp, ch 1, [shell in next ch-1 sp, ch 1] 4 times, rep from * around, join in top of beg ch-3. *(6 corner shells, 24 shells)*

Rnd 7: Sl st in next dc and ch-1 sp, beg corner shell in same sp, ch 1, [shell in next ch-1 sp, ch 1] 5 times, *corner shell in next corner ch-1 sp, ch 1, [shell in next

ch-1 sp, ch 1] 5 times, rep from * around, join in top of beg ch-3. Fasten off. *(6 corner shells, 30 shells)*

Rnd 8: Join B in any corner ch-1 sp, beg corner shell in same sp, place marker in center ch of corner shell just made, dc in next ch-1 sp, ch 14, sk next 4 ch-1 sps, dc in next ch-1 sp, *corner shell in next corner ch-1 sp, shell in each ch-1 sp across to corner, rep from * around, join in top of beg ch-3. Fasten off. *(6 corner shells, 2 dc, 30 shells)*

Rnd 9: Join E in marked corner ch-1 sp, beg corner shell in same sp, sk next 2 dc of corner shell, dc in next dc, dc in each of 14 chs, dc in next dc, corner shell in next corner ch-1 sp, sk next dc of corner shell, dc in next dc of corner shell, dc in each of next 6 dc, place marker in st just made, dc in each of next 6 dc, dc in first dc of corner shell, *corner shell in next corner ch-1 sp, sk next dc of corner shell, dc in next dc of corner shell, dc in each of next 12 dc, dc in first dc of corner shell, rep from * twice, corner shell in next corner ch-1 sp, sk next dc of corner shell, dc in next dc of corner shell, dc in each of next 7 dc, place marker in st just made, dc in each of next 5 dc, dc in first dc of corner shell, join in top of beg ch-3. Fasten off. *(6 corner shells, 86 dc)*

Finishing

Hold Front and Back tog with RS facing outward and join E in top left marked st of both pieces. Working through both thicknesses, sc pieces tog, working around side and bottom edges to rem marked st. Fasten off. ●

Tulipan Doily

Design by Monica Mance

Skill Level

 INTERMEDIATE

Finished Measurement

8 inches in diameter from point to point

Materials

- Omega size 10 crochet cotton (173 yds per ball):
  1 ball #154 pistachio
- Size B/1/2.25mm crochet hook or size needed to obtain gauge
- Locking stitch markers: 9

0 LACE

Gauge

Diameter after rnd 2: 2¼ inches

Take time to check gauge.

Pattern Notes

Weave in loose ends as work progresses.

Join with slip stitch as indicated unless otherwise stated.

The rounds with bobbles are crocheted on the wrong side of the piece. All other rounds are crocheted with the right side facing.

Move marker up to first stitch of each round as work progresses.

Chain-4 at beginning of round counts as first treble crochet unless otherwise stated.

After working into first half double crochet at each peak of rounds 7 and 8, it may be helpful to place a stitch marker in 2nd half double crochet of each peak. In this case, you will need 8 additional markers for round 8.

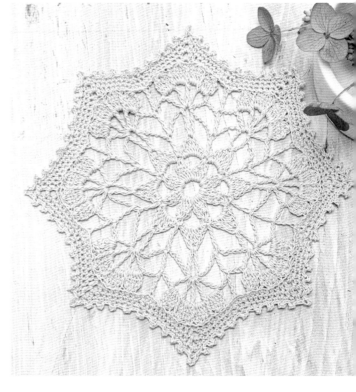

Special Stitches

5-treble bobble (bobble): [Yo twice, insert hook into indicated sp, yo, pull up a lp, {yo, pull through 2 lps} twice] 5 times in same sp, yo and draw through all 6 lps on hook.

Picot: Ch 3, sl st into back bar of 3rd ch from hook.

Picot

Doily

Rnd 1 (WS): Ch 8, taking care to not twist the ch, **join** *(see Pattern Notes)* under both lps of 8th ch from hook to form a ring. Place **marker** *(see Pattern Notes)* in top of first bobble of the rnd. Ch 4 *(counts as first leg of bobble)*, [**bobble** *(see Special Stitches)*, ch 3] 8 times in ring, join by removing lp from hook, keeping the lp open, turn to have RS facing, insert hook, front to back, into top of first bobble under both lps, without twisting the ch, put lp back on hook, pull lp through the st. *(8 bobbles)*

Rnd 2 (RS): Ch 1, *(sl st, ch 1, sc, hdc, dc, tr, ch 1, tr, dc, hdc, sc, ch 1, sl st) in next ch-3 sp; rep from * 7 times, join in beg ch-1. *(16 sl sts, 24 ch-1 sps, 16 sc, 16 hdc, 16 dc, 16 tr)*

Rnd 3 (RS): Ch 4 *(see Pattern Notes)*, *ch 6, sk next ch-1 sp, (tr, ch 2, tr) in next ch-1 sp *(at peak)*, ch 6**, sk next ch-1 sp and following sl st, tr in next sl st; rep from * around, ending last rep at **, join in 4th ch of beg ch-4. *(24 tr, 16 ch-6 sps, 8 ch-2 sps)*

Rnd 4 (RS): Ch 4, *ch 3, sk ch-6 sp, ([tr, ch 2] 4 times, tr) in next ch-2 sp, ch 3, sk next ch-6 sp**, tr in next tr; rep from * around, ending last rep at **, join in 4th ch of beg ch-4, turn. *(48 tr, 32 ch-2 sps, 16 ch-3 sps)*

Rnd 5 (WS): Ch 4, *ch 3, sk next ch-3 sp, [bobble in next ch-2 sp, ch 1, **bptr** *(see Stitch Guide)* around next tr, ch 1] 3 times, bobble in next ch-2 sp, ch 3, sk next ch-3 sp**, tr in next tr; rep from * around, ending last rep at **, join in 4th ch of beg ch-4, move marker to **front lp** *(see Stitch Guide)* of sl st, turn. *(32 bobbles, 24 bptr, 8 tr, 48 ch-1 sps, 16 ch-3 sps)*

Rnd 6 (RS): Working all sts in **back lps** *(see Stitch Guide)*, sc in marked lp of sl st, *sc in each of next 3 chs, sc in next bobble, sc in next ch-1 sp, sc in next bptr, sc in next ch-1 sp, sc in next bobble, sc in next ch-1 sp, (hdc, ch 2, hdc) in next bptr, sc in next ch-1 sp, sc in next bobble, sc in next ch-1 sp, sc in next bptr, sc in next ch-1 sp, sc in next bobble, sc in each of next 3 chs**, sc in next tr; rep from * around, ending last rep at **, join under both lps of beg sc. *(152 sc, 16 hdc, 8 ch-2 sps)*

Rnd 7 (RS): Ch 1, sc in same sc as join, ***sc dec** *(see Stitch Guide)* in next 2 sc, sc in each of next 7 sc, sc in **next hdc** *(see Pattern Notes)*, (hdc, ch 2, hdc) in next ch-2 sp, sc in next hdc, sc in each of next 7 sc, sc dec in next 2 sc**, sc in next sc; rep from * around, ending last rep at **, join in beg sc. *(152 sc, 16 hdc, 2 ch-2 sps)*

Rnd 8 (RS): Rep rnd 7, placing markers in each sc which is in between 2 sc dec *(8 markers placed)*.

Rnd 9 (RS): Picot *(see Special Stitches)*, *sl st in next sc, sc dec in next 2 sc, picot, [sl st in next 2 sc, picot] 3 times, sl st in next hdc, (sl st, picot) in ch-2 sp, sl st in next hdc, sl st in next sc, picot, [sl st in next 2 sc, picot] twice, sl st in next sc, sc dec in next 2 sc, picot, sl st in next sc**, sl st, picot in marked sc; rep from * around ending last rep at **, join in base of beg picot. Fasten off.

Finishing
Wet-block to finished size. ●

With Love Coaster

Design by Cherie Bernatt of Crochet Mon Cherie

Skill Level

 INTERMEDIATE

Finished Measurement

4½ inches in diameter

Materials

- Aunt Lydia's Fashion Crochet size 3 crochet cotton (150 yds per ball):
    - 1 ball #6 scarlet
- Size B/1/2.25mm crochet hook or size needed to obtain gauge
- Tapestry needle

Gauge

Rnds 1 and 2 = 1¾ inches in diameter

Pattern Notes

Weave in loose ends as work progresses.

Join with slip stitch as indicated unless otherwise stated.

Chain-3 at beginning of round counts as first double crochet unless otherwise stated.

Special Stitches

2-double crochet cluster (2-dc cl): Yo, insert hook in indicated st, yo, pull up a lp, yo, draw through 2 lps on hook *(2 lps on hook)*, yo, insert hook in same st, yo, pull up a lp, yo, draw through 2 lps on hook *(3 lps on hook)*, yo, draw through all 3 lps on hook.

Double crochet 2 stitches together (dc2tog): [Yo, insert hook in next st, yo and pull up a lp, yo, draw through 2 lps] twice, yo, draw through all 3 lps on hook.

Coaster

Ch 8, **join** *(see Pattern Notes)* in first ch to form a ring.

Rnd 1: Ch 3 *(see Pattern Notes)*, 23 dc in ring, join in top of beg ch-3. *(24 dc)*

Rnd 2: Ch 3, dc in next st, ch 4, *sk next st, dc in each of next 2 sts, ch 4; rep from * around, sk next st, join in top of beg ch-3. *(16 dc)*

Rnd 3: Ch 3, dc in next st, ch 5, *sk next sp, dc in each of next 2 sts, ch 5; rep from * around, sk next sp, join in top of beg ch-3. *(16 dc, 40 chs)*

Rnd 4: Ch 3, dc in same st as join, 2 dc in next st, *ch 2, sk next 2 chs, dc in next ch, ch 2, sk next 2 chs**, 2 dc in each of next 2 dc; rep from * around, ending last rep at **, join in top of beg ch-3. *(40 dc)*

Rnd 5: Ch 3, dc in same st as join, ***2-dc cl** *(see Special Stitches)* in each of next 2 sts, 2 dc in next st, ch 2, dc in next dc, ch 2**, 2 dc in next dc; rep from * around, ending last rep at **, join in top of beg ch-3. *(40 dc, 16 2-dc cls)*

Rnd 6: *Ch 3, **dc2tog** *(see Special Stitches)*, ch 2, sl st in last st worked, sl st in next st, ch 3, dc2tog, ch 2, sl

st in last st worked, ch 2, sk next sp, sc in next dc, ch 2, sk next sp, sl st in next st, rep from * around, join in top of beg ch-3, finish off. *(8 sc, 16 dc)*

Finishing
Block as needed and starch, if desired. ●

Double-Flower Dishcloth

Design by Kristen Stoltzfus Clay

Skill Level
 INTERMEDIATE

Finished Measurement
7¾ inches at widest point

Materials
- Lily Sugar'n Cream medium (worsted) weight cotton yarn (2½ oz/120 yds/71g per ball):
    1 ball each #01699 tangerine and #01004 soft ecru
- Size H/8/5mm crochet hook or size needed to obtain gauge
- Yarn needle

Gauge
Rnds 1 and 2 = 3 inches

Pattern Notes
Weave in loose ends as work progresses.

Join with slip stitch as indicated unless otherwise stated.

Chain-2 at beginning of round does not count as first stitch unless otherwise stated.

Special Stitches
2-double crochet cluster (2-dc cl): [Yo, insert hook in indicated st, yo, draw up a lp, yo, draw through 2 lps on hook] twice in same st *(3 lps on hook)*, yo, draw through all lps on hook.

V-stitch (V-st): (Dc, ch 2, dc) in indicated st.

Popcorn (pc): 4 tr in indicated st, draw up lp, remove hook, insert hook in first tr of 4-tr group, pick up dropped lp and draw through st on hook.

Dishcloth

Rnd 1 (RS): Beg at center with tangerine, ch 7, **join** (see Pattern Notes) in first ch to form ring, **ch 2** (see Pattern Notes), [3 dc in ring, ch 1] 6 times, join in first dc. (18 dc)

Rnd 2: Ch 2, [**2-dc cl** (see Special Stitches) in first dc, (dc, ch 1, dc) in next dc, 2-dc cl in next dc, ch 1] around, join in first 2-dc cl. (12 2-dc cls, 12 dc, 12 ch-1 sps)

Rnd 3: Ch 2, [2-dc cl in first 2-dc cl, **V-st** (see Special Stitches) in ch-1 sp between dc sts, 2-dc cl in next 2-dc cl, sk next ch-1 sp, ch 2] around, join in first 2-dc cl.

Rnd 4: Ch 2, [2-dc cl in first 2-dc cl, dc in next dc of V-st, V-st in ch-2 sp of V-st, dc in next dc of V-st, 2-dc cl in next 2-dc cl, ch 2] around, join in first 2-dc cl. (12 2-dc cls, 24 dc, 12 ch-2 sps)

Rnd 5: Ch 1, [sc in first 2-dc cl, (3 tr, **pc**—see Special Stitches, 3 tr) in ch-2 sp of V-st, sc in next 2-dc cl, 3 tr in next ch-2 sp] around, join in first sc. Fasten off. (6 pc, 36 tr, 30 sc)

Edging

Join soft ecru in next tr, ch 1, [hdc in each of next 3 tr, (hdc, 2 dc, hdc) in top of pc, hdc in each of next 3 tr, sc in next 2 sc, sk next sc, working on RS, **dtr** (see Stitch Guide) in ch-1 sp of rnd 2 directly below, sc in next 2 sc] around, join in first hdc. Fasten off. (6 dtr, 12 dc, 24 sc, 48 hdc)

Flower

Rnd 1: With soft ecru, form a **slip ring** (see illustration), ch 1, (sc, ch 2, 3 tr, ch 2) 6 times in ring, join in first sc, pull loose end to tighten ring. (18 tr)

Rnd 2: Sl st in first ch-2 sp, ch 1, [sc in ch-2 sp, sc in next tr, 3 hdc in next tr, sc in next tr, sc in ch-2 sp] around, join in first sc. Fasten off. (18 hdc, 24 sc)

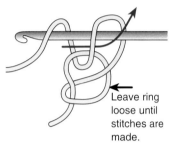

Leave ring loose until stitches are made.

Slip Ring

Finishing

Position Flower in center of Dishcloth, working through both thicknesses with tangerine, sl st Flower to Dishcloth working through sts of rnd 2 of Flower, join in first sl st. Fasten off. ●

Round & Round Mini Throw

Design by Kathleen Berlew

Skill Level
■■□□ EASY

Finished Measurement
31 inches in diameter

Materials
- Bernat Super Value medium (worsted) weight acrylic yarn (7 oz/426 yds/197g per skein):
  1 skein #7414 natural
- Size K/10½/6.5mm crochet hook or size needed to obtain gauge
- Tapestry needle

Gauge

3 rnds = 3 inches

Pattern Notes

Weave in loose ends as work progresses.

Join with slip stitch as indicated unless otherwise stated.

If desired, add an alternate scrap color on any round.

Special Stitches

Beginning 2-treble cluster (beg 2-tr cl): Ch 3, tr in indicated st or sp.

2-treble crochet cluster (2-tr cl): Yo twice, insert hook in indicated st or sp, yo, draw up a lp, [yo, draw through 2 lps on hook] twice, yo twice, insert hook in same st or sp, draw up a lp, [yo, draw through 2 lps on hook] twice, yo, draw through all 3 lps on hook.

Beginning V-stitch cluster (beg V-cl): (Ch 3, tr, ch 2, 2-tr cl) in indicated st or sp.

V-stitch cluster (V-cl): (2-tr cl, ch 2, 2-tr cl) in indicated st or sp.

Throw

Rnd 1 (RS): Ch 5, **join** (see Pattern Notes) in beg ch to form a ring, **beg 2-tr cl** (see Special Stitches) in ring, ch 3, [**2-tr cl** (see Special Stitches), ch 3] 7 times in ring, join in beg 2-tr cl. (8 2-tr cls)

Rnd 2: Sl st in next ch-3 sp, **beg V-cl** (see Special Stitches) in same sp, ch 2, ***V-cl** (see Special Stitches) in next ch-3 sp, ch 2, rep from * around, join in beg V-cl. (8 V-cls)

Rnd 3: Sl st in next ch-2 sp, beg V-cl in same sp, ch 2, 2-tr cl in next ch-2 sp, ch 2, *V-cl in next V-cl, ch 2, 2-tr cl in next ch-2 sp, ch 2, rep from * around, join in beg V-cl. (8 V-cls, 8 2-tr cls)

Rnd 4: Sl st in next ch-2 sp, beg V-cl in same sp, ch 2, V-st cl in next 2-tr cl, ch 2, *V-cl in next V-cl, ch 2, V-cl in next 2-tr cl, ch 2, rep from * around, join in beg V-cl. (16 V-cls)

Rnd 5: Rep rnd 3. (16 V-cls, 16 2-tr cls)

Rnd 6: Sl st in next ch-2 sp, beg V-cl in same sp, [ch 1, tr in next ch sp] twice, ch 1, *V-cl in next V-cl, [ch 1, tr in next ch sp] twice, ch 1, rep from * around, join in beg V-cl. (16 V-cls, 32 tr)

Rnd 7: Sl st in next ch-2 sp, beg V-cl in same sp, [ch 1, tr in next ch-1 sp] 3 times, ch 1, *V-cl in next V-cl, [ch 1, tr in next ch-1 sp] 3 times, ch 1, rep from * around, join in beg V-cl. (1 beg V-cl, 15 V-cls, 48 tr)

Rnd 8: Sl st in next ch-2 sp, beg V-cl in same sp, ch 1, sk next ch-1 sp, tr and ch sp, V-cl in next tr, ch 1, *V-cl in next V-cl, ch 1, sk next ch sp, tr and ch sp, V-cl in next tr, ch 1, rep from * around, join in beg V-cl. (32 V-cls)

Rnd 9: Sl st in next ch-2 sp, beg V-cl in same sp, ch 1, 2-tr cl in next ch-1 sp, ch 1, 2-tr cl in next V-cl, ch 1, 2-tr cl in next ch-1 sp, ch 1, *V-cl in next V-cl, ch 1, 2-tr cl in next ch-1 sp, ch 1, 2-tr cl in next V-cl, ch 1, 2-tr cl in next ch-1 sp, ch 1, rep from * around, join in beg V-cl. (16 V-cls, 48 2-tr cls)

Rnd 10: Sl st in next ch-2 sp, beg V-cl in same sp, ch 1, [tr in next ch sp, ch 1] 4 times, *V-cl in next V-cl, ch 1, [tr in next ch sp, ch 1] 4 times, rep from * around, join in beg V-cl. (15 V-cls, 64 tr)

Rnd 11: Sl st in next ch-2 sp, beg V-cl in same sp, ch 1, [sk next ch sp, V-cl in next ch sp, ch 1] twice, *V-cl in next V-cl, ch 1, [sk next ch sp, V-cl in next ch sp, ch 1] twice, rep from * around, join in beg V-cl. *(1 beg V-cl, 47 V-cls)*

Rnd 12: Sl st in next ch-2 sp, beg V-cl in same sp, ch 1, 2-tr cl in next ch sp, ch 1, [2-tr cl in next V-cl, ch 1, 2-tr cl in next ch sp, ch 1] twice, *V-cl in next V-cl, ch 1, 2-tr cl in next ch sp, ch 1, [2-tr cl in next V-cl, ch 1, 2-tr cl in next ch sp, ch 1] twice, rep from * around, join in beg V-cl. *(16 V-cls, 80 2-tr cls)*

Rnd 13: Sl st in next ch-2 sp, beg V-cl in same sp, ch 1, [tr in next ch sp, ch 1] 6 times, *V-cl in next V-cl, ch 1, [tr in next ch sp, ch 1] 6 times, rep from * around, join in beg V-cl. *(16 V-cls, 96 tr)*

Rnd 14: Sl st in next ch-2 sp, beg V-cl in same sp, ch 1, [sk next ch sp, V-cl in next ch sp, ch 1] 3 times, *V-cl in next V-cl, ch 1, [sk next ch sp, V-cl in next ch sp, ch 1] 3 times, rep from * around, join in beg V-cl. *(64 V-cls)*

Rnd 15: Sl st in next ch-2 sp, ch 1, 2 sc in same sp, ch 1, sc in next ch sp, ch 1, [2 sc in next ch-2 sp, ch 1, sc in next ch sp] around, join in beg sc. Fasten off. *(192 sc)* ●

Barista Cowl

Design by Kathleen Berlew

Skill Level

 EASY

Finished Measurements

16 inches wide x 52½ inches in circumference

Materials

- Premier Yarns Anti-Pilling Everyday DK light (DK) weight acrylic yarn (3½ oz/273 yds/ 100g per ball):
    2 balls #1107-30 charcoal (A)
    1 ball each #1107-14 teal (B) and
    #1107-24 mist (C)

- Size G/6/4mm crochet hook or size needed to obtain gauge
- Tapestry needle

Gauge

15 sts = 4 inches; rows 1–6 = 3¾ inches

Pattern Notes

Cowl is worked in turned rows and joined at short ends.

Weave in loose ends as work progresses.

Chain-4 at beginning of row counts as first treble crochet unless otherwise stated.

Chain-3 at beginning of row counts as first double crochet unless otherwise stated.

Chain-2 at beginning of round counts as first half double crochet unless otherwise stated.

Join with slip stitch as indicated unless otherwise stated.

Special Stitches

Shell: 3 dc in indicated st.

Cluster (cl): Yo, insert hook in indicated st, pull up a lp, yo, draw through 2 lps on hook *(2 lps on hook)*, [yo, insert hook in same st, pull up a lp, yo, draw through 2 lps] twice *(4 lps on hook)*, yo, draw through all 4 lps on hook.

A

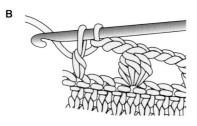

B

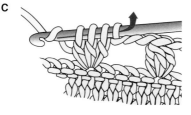

C

Cluster

Cowl

Row 1 (RS): With A, ch 63, working in **back bars** *(see illustration)*, tr in 5th ch from hook *(beg 4 sk chs count as first tr)* and in each ch across, turn. *(60 tr)*

Back Bar of Chain

Row 2: Ch 4 *(see Pattern Notes)*, tr in each st across, **change color** *(see Stitch Guide)* to B, turn.

Row 3: Ch 3 *(see Pattern Notes)*, dc in next st, [ch 1, sk next st, dc in next st] across to last 2 sts, dc in last 2 sts, turn. *(32 dc, 28 ch sps)*

Row 4: Ch 3, dc in next 2 dc, [**shell** *(see Special Stitches)* in next dc, dc in next dc] across to last st, dc in last st, turn. *(14 shells, 18 dc)*

Row 5: Ch 3, dc in next dc, [ch 1, **dc dec** *(see Stitch Guide)* in each dc of next shell, ch 1, dc in next dc] across to last 2 sts, dc in last 2 sts, turn. *(14 dc dec, 18 dc, 28 ch sps)*

Row 6: Ch 3, dc in next 2 dc, [ch 1, dc in next dc dec, ch 1, dc in next dc] across to last st, dc in last st, change color to A, turn. *(32 dc, 28 ch sps)*

Row 7: Ch 4, tr in each st and sp across, turn. *(60 tr)*

Row 8: Rep row 2, change color to C.

Row 9: Rep row 3.

Row 10: Ch 3, dc in next dc, [ch 1, sk next dc, **cl** *(see Special Stitches)* in next ch sp] across, to last 2 sts, ch 1, sk next st, dc in last st, turn. *(28 cls, 3 dc, 29 ch sps)*

Row 11: Ch 3, dc in first ch sp, [ch 1, cl in next ch sp] across to last 2 sts, ch 1, sk next dc, dc in last st, turn.

Row 12: Ch 3, dc in next ch sp, [ch 1, sk next cl, dc in next ch sp] across to last 2 sts, dc in last 2 sts, change color to A, turn.

Rows 13 & 14: Rep rows 7 and 8, change color to B, turn.

Rows 15–74: [Rep rows 3–14] 5 times in established color sequence.

Rows 75–84: Rep rows 3–12. At end of row 84, fasten off, leaving a long tail for sewing.

Finishing

Sew short edges of Cowl tog.

Border

With RS facing and working in ends of rows, **join** (see Pattern Notes) B in any dc row on either edge of Cowl, **ch 2** (see Pattern Notes), hdc in same row, hdc around, working 2 hdc in end of each dc row and 3 hdc in end of each tr row, join in top of beg ch-2, fasten off. Rep around rem edge. ●

Ring of Roses Coasters & Basket

Designs by Laurie Ann Sand

Skill Level

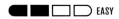 EASY

Finished Measurements

Coaster: 4 inches square

Basket: 4¼ inches square x 2¼ inches tall

Materials

- Lily Sugar'n Cream Super Size Ombré medium (worsted) weight cotton yarn (3 oz/150 yds/ 85g per ball):
    1 ball #919144 strawberry
- Lily Sugar'n Cream Super Size Scents medium (worsted) weight cotton yarn (3 oz/150 yds/ 85g per ball):
    1 ball #525222 aloe vera
- Size J/10/6mm crochet hook or size needed to obtain gauge
- Tapestry needle
- Stitch marker

Gauge

Rnds 1–4 = 4 inches square

Pattern Notes

Coaster and Basket are worked with right side facing at all times.

Weave in loose ends as work progresses.

Join with slip stitch as indicated unless otherwise stated.

Special Stitches

Leaves and stems (L&S): (Sc, [ch 8, sc] 3 times) in indicated st.

Rosebud: Inserting hook from front to back in center ch-8 sp of next L&S, 6 dc in next sc.

Coaster

Make 4: 2 with strawberry as color A and aloe vera as color B, and 2 with aloe vera as color A and strawberry as color B.

With color A, make a **slip ring** (see illustration).

Rnd 1: Ch 5 (counts as first dc and ch 2), [dc, ch 2] 7 times in ring, pull tail to close ring, **join** (see Pattern Notes) in 3rd ch of beg ch-5, finish off. (8 dc, 8 ch-2 sps)

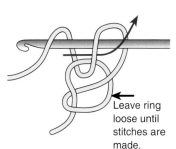

4" end

Leave ring loose until stitches are made.

Slip Ring

Rnd 2: Join color B in any ch-2 sp, ch 1, sc in same sp, 7 dc in next ch-2 sp, [sc in next ch-2 sp, 7 dc

in next ch-2 sp] around, join in beg sc, finish off. *(4 sc, 28 dc)*

Rnd 3: Join color A in any sc, ch 3 *(counts as first dc)*, 4 dc in same st, sk next 3 dc, 7 dc in next dc, [sk next 3 dc, 5 dc in next sc, sk next 3 dc, 7 dc in next dc] around, join in 3rd ch of beg ch-3, finish off. *(4 7-dc groups, 20 dc)*

Rnd 4: Join color B in center dc of any 7-dc group, ch 1, 3 sc in same st, sc in next 11 sts, [3 sc in next st *(center st of current 7-dc group)*, sc in next 11 sts] around, join in beg sc, finish off. *(56 sc)*

Finishing
Block to finished measurements, if desired.

Basket

Rnds 1–4: With aloe vera as color A and strawberry as color B, work same as rnds 1–4 of Coaster, do not finish off at end of rnd 4.

Rnd 5: Ch 1, sc in same sc as join, 3 sc in next sc, [sc in next 13 sc, 3 sc in next sc] 3 times, sc in last 12 sc,

join in beg sc. Place marker in center sc between any 2 groups of 3 sc, move up as each rnd is completed. *(64 sc)*

Rnd 6: Ch 1, working in **back lps** *(see Stitch Guide)*, sc in same sc as join and in each sc around, join in beg sc.

Rnd 7: Ch 1, sc in same sc as join and in each sc around, join in beg sc of rnd, finish off.

Rnd 8: Join color A in marked sc, ch 1, sc in same sc, sc in next 6 sc, **L&S** *(see Special Stitches)* in next sc, [sc in next 9 sc, L&S in next sc] 5 times, sc in last 6 sc, join in beg sc, finish off. *(76 sc, 18 ch-8 sps)*

Rnd 9: Join color B in first sc, ch 1, sc in same sc, sc in next 6 sc, [ch 1, sk next L&S*, sc in next 9 sc] 6 times, ending last rep at *, sc in last 6 sc, join in beg sc. *(58 sc, 6 chs)*

Rnd 10: Ch 1, sc in same sc as join, sc in next 3 sc, [inserting hook from front to back in first ch-8 sp of next L&S, sc in next sc, sc in next 2 sc, sc in next ch *(not in ch-1 sp)*, sc in next 2 sc, inserting hook from front to back in last ch-8 sp of same L&S, sc in next sc, sc in next 3 sc] 6 times, join in beg sc. *(64 sc)*

Rnd 11: Ch 1, sc in same sc as join and in each sc around, join in beg sc.

Rnd 12: Ch 1, sc in same sc as join and in next 6 sc, [**rosebud** *(see Special Stitches)*, sc in next 9 sc] 5 times, rosebud, sc in last 6 sc, join in beg sc. *(58 sc, 36 dc)*

Rnd 13: Ch 1, sc in same sc as join and in next 6 sc, [ch 1, sk next rosebud, sc in next 9 sc] 5 times, ch 1, sk last rosebud, sc in last 6 sc, join in beg sc. *(58 sc, 6 ch-1 sps)*

Rnd 14: Ch 1, sc in same sc as join and in each sc and ch-1 sp around, join in beg sc of rnd, finish off. *(64 sc)*

Finishing
Block to measurements, if desired, being careful not to flatten rosebuds. ●

California Coast Beanie

Design by Lena Skvagerson for Annie's Signature Designs

Skill Level

 BEGINNER

Finished Sizes

Instructions given fit size small/medium; changes for large/X-large are in [ ].

Finished Measurements

Circumference: 20½ inches *(small/medium)* [22½ inches *(large/X-large)*], with 2–3 inches of stretch

Length: 9 inches *(small/medium)* [10 inches *(large/X-large)*]

Materials

- Berroco Vintage medium (worsted) weight acrylic/wool/nylon yarn (3½ oz/217 yds/100g per hank):
    1 hank each #5189 charcoal and #5145 cast iron
- Size H/8/5mm crochet hook or size needed to obtain gauge
- Tapestry needle
- Stitch marker

Gauge

14 sc = 4 inches; 16 sc rnds = 4 inches

Pattern Notes

Weave in loose ends as work progresses.

Join with slip stitch as indicated unless otherwise stated.

Do not join rounds unless otherwise stated. Use stitch marker to mark rounds and move as work progresses.

Beanie

Rnd 1: Beg at center top of Beanie, with charcoal, ch 4, **join** *(see Pattern Notes)* to form a ring, 8 sc in ring, place **stitch marker** *(see Pattern Notes)*.

Rnd 2: Working in **back lp** *(see Stitch Guide)* of each st throughout, 2 sc in each sc around. *(16 sc)*

Rnd 3: [Sc in next sc, 2 sc in next sc] around. *(24 sc)*

Rnd 4: [Sc in each of next 2 sc, 2 sc in next sc] around. *(32 sc)*

Rnd 5: [Sc in each of next 3 sc, 2 sc in next sc] around. *(40 sc)*

Rnd 6: [Sc in each of next 4 sc, 2 sc in next sc] around. *(48 sc)*

Rnd 7: [Sc in each of next 5 sc, 2 sc in next sc] around. *(56 sc)*

Rnd 8: [Sc in each of next 6 sc, 2 sc in next sc] around. *(64 sc)*

Rnd 9: [Sc in each of next 7 sc, 2 sc in next sc] around. *(72 sc)*

Rnd 10: [Sc in each of next 8 sc, 2 sc in next sc] around. *(80 sc)*

Size Large/X-Large Only

Rnd [11]: [Sc in each of next 9 sc, 2 sc in next sc] around. *([88] sc)*

Both Sizes

Rnd 11 [12]: Sc in each of next 80 [88] sts around.

Rep rnd 11 [12] until Beanie measures 6 [7] inches.

Bottom Border

Both Sizes

Rnd 1: Draw up a lp of cast iron, drop charcoal to WS, sc in each st around to last st, **change color** *(see Stitch Guide)* to charcoal, drop cast iron to WS. *(80 [88] sc)*

Rnd 2: Sc in each sc around to last sc, change color to cast iron, drop charcoal to WS.

Rnds 3 & 4: Sc in each sc around to last sc, at the end of last rep, change color to charcoal, drop cast iron to WS.

Rnds 5 & 6: Sc in each sc around to last sc, **do not fasten off**.

Rnd 7: Continuing with charcoal, *sc dec *(see Stitch Guide)* in next 2 sts, sc in each of next 8 [9] sts, rep from * around, change color to cast iron, fasten off charcoal. *(72 [80] sc)*

Rnds 8–12: Sc in each st around. At the end of last rep, sl st in next st. Fasten off. ●

Hampshire Pocket Scarf

Design by Alexandra Tavel/Two of Wands

Skill Level

 INTERMEDIATE

Finished Measurements

16 inches wide x 59½ inches long

Materials

- Lion Brand Hue + Me bulky (chunky) weight acrylic/wool yarn (4.4 oz/137 yds/125g per ball):
    6 balls #132 arrowwood
- Size N/P/15/10mm crochet hook or size needed to obtain gauge
- Tapestry needle

Gauge

8 HBhdc = 4 inches; 7 rows = 4 inches

Take time to check gauge.

Pattern Notes

Weave in loose ends as work progresses.

To adjust length for the perfect fit, measure your wingspan from fingertip to fingertip. Subtract 4 inches for drag/stretch when worn. This measurement is the length to make your wrap. Add or subtract 2 stitches for every inch you would like to shorten or lengthen the wrap.

Special Stitches

Herringbone half double crochet (HBhdc): Yo, insert hook into indicated st, draw up a lp and pull through first lp on hook (*as a sl st*), yo, draw through both lps on hook.

Puff stitch (PS): Yo, insert hook into indicated st (*see illustration A*), draw up a lp (*3 lps on hook, see illustration B*), yo, insert hook into same st, draw up a lp (*5 lps on hook, see illustration C*), yo, insert hook into same st, draw up a lp (*7 lps on hook*), yo, draw through all lps on hook (*see illustration D*).

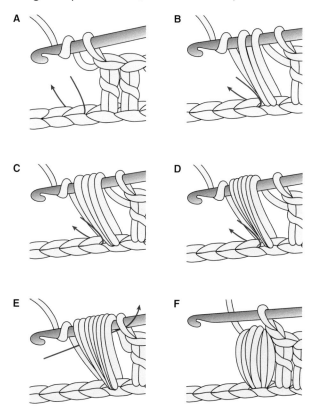

Puff Stitch

Scarf

Row 1 (RS): Ch 120 (*see Pattern Notes*), **HBhdc** (*see Special Stitches*) in 2nd ch from hook and in each rem ch across, turn. (*119 HBhdc*)

Rows 2–18: Ch 1, HBhdc in each st across, turn.

Edging

Row 19: Ch 1, hdc in first st, **PS** (*see Special Stitches*) in next st, *ch 1, sk 1 st, PS in next st; rep from * to last st, hdc in last st, turn. (*59 PS, 58 ch-1 sps, 2 hdc*)

Row 20: Ch 1, hdc in first st, ch 1, *PS in next ch sp, ch 1; rep from * to last st, hdc in last st, turn. (*58 PS, 59 ch-1 sps, 2 hdc*)

Note: *Work the following rows loosely to ensure fabric doesn't shrink and pucker.*

Row 21: Ch 1, sc in each st and ch-1 sp across, turn. (*119 sc*)

Row 22: Sl st in each st across, turn.

Row 23: Ch 1, sc in each st across, turn.

Row 24: Rep row 22.

Fasten off.

Rotate work and with RS facing, rejoin yarn to first foundation ch, working across the other side of the foundation ch to beg, rep rows 19–24. Fasten off.

Pocket

Make 2.

Row 1 (RS): Ch 22, HBhdc in 2nd ch from hook and in each rem ch across, turn. *(21 HBhdc)*

Rows 2–14: Ch 1, HBhdc in each st across, turn.

Edging

Row 15: Rep row 19 of scarf edging. *(10 PS, 9 ch-1 sps, 2 hdc)*

Row 16: Rep row 20 of scarf edging. *(9 PS, 10 ch-1 sps, 2 hdc)*

Rows 17–20: Rep rows 21–24 of scarf edging. *(21 sts)*

Fasten off.

Finishing

Place the pockets at each end of the wrap so that the sides of the pockets line up with the edging *(just within the PS rows)* and bottoms align with the short edges of scarf. Sew pockets in place using a **whipstitch** *(see illustration)* along the sides and bottom edge. ●

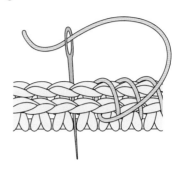

Whipstitch Edges

Four Paws Coasters

Design by Lisa McDonald

Skill Level

 EASY

Finished Measurement

4 inches square

Materials

- Scheepjes Softfun light (DK) weight cotton/acrylic yarn (1¾ oz/153 yds/50g per ball): 1 ball each #2530 cloud and #2601 graphite
- Size F/5/3.75mm crochet hook or size needed to obtain gauge
- Tapestry needle

Gauge

11 sc = 2 inches; 11 rows = 2 inches

Pattern Notes

Coaster is worked from written instructions and Chart in 2 contrasting colors with tapestry crochet technique. Instructions given are for graphite as main color and cloud as contrast color; changes for cloud as main color and graphite as contrast color are in [ ].

Weave in loose ends as work progresses.

When changing color, carry and work over color not in use on wrong side of piece. Do not cut or fasten off colors until work with each color is complete.

Each Chart square depicts 1 single crochet; refer to Key for color changes. Odd-numbered, right-side rows are read from right to left; even-numbered, wrong-side rows are read from left to right.

Join with slip stitch as indicated unless otherwise stated.

Coaster

Make 2 each graphite/cloud and cloud/graphite.

Row 1 (RS): With graphite [cloud], ch 20, sc in 2nd ch from hook and in each rem ch across, turn. *(19 sc)*

Row 2: Ch 1, sc in each sc across, turn.

Row 3: Ch 1, sc in each of first 5 sc, **changing color** *(see Pattern Notes and Stitch Guide)* to cloud [graphite] in last sc, sc in each of next 3 sc, change color to graphite [cloud], sc in each of next 3 sc, changing to cloud [graphite], sc in each of next 3 sc, change color to graphite [cloud], sc in each of last 5 sc, turn. *(13 graphite [cloud] sc, 6 cloud [graphite] sc)*

Row 4: Ch 1, sc in each of first 4 sc, change color to cloud [graphite], sc in each of next 5 sc, changing color to graphite [cloud], sc in next sc, change color to cloud [graphite], sc in each of next 5 sc, change color to graphite [cloud], sc in each of last 4 sc, turn. *(9 graphite [cloud] sc, 10 cloud [graphite] sc)*

Rows 5–19: Referring to **Chart** *(see Chart and Pattern Notes)*, sc in each sc across, changing color as indicated, turn. At end of last row, do not fasten off graphite [cloud]. Cut cloud [graphite].

Finishing

Rnd 1 (WS): With WS facing, ch 1, 2 sc in first sc, sc in each of next 17 sc, *3 sc in last sc *(corner made)*, working in ends of rows across side, work 17 sc evenly to next corner*, 3 sc in next corner, working in opposite side of foundation ch, sc in next 17 chs, rep between *, sc in same sc as beg 2 sc, **join** *(see Pattern Notes)* in beg sc. Fasten off. *(80 sc: 68 sc [17 sc across each side], 4 groups of 3 sc)*

Note: *In 1 graphite [cloud] Coaster, work rnd 2 with same color; in rem graphite [cloud] Coaster, work rnd 2 with cloud [graphite].*

Rnd 2: With RS facing, join yarn in 3rd sc of any 3-sc group, ch 1, sc in same sc, *sc in each sc around to center st of next 3-sc group, 3 sc in center st, rep from * around, join in beg sc. Fasten off. *(88 sc: 76 sc [19 sc across each side], 4 groups of 3 sc)* ●

COLOR KEY
☐ Cloud
■ Graphite

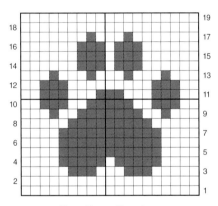

Four Paws Coasters
Chart 1

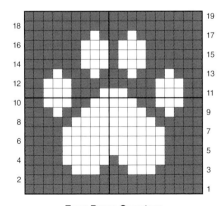

Four Paws Coasters
Chart 2

Top-Down Baby Cardi

Design by Lena Skvagerson for Annie's Signature Designs

Skill Level

 EASY

Finished Sizes

Instructions given to fit baby size 0–3 months; sizes 6–9 months, 9–12 months and 18–24 months are in [ ]. When only 1 number is given, it applies to all sizes.

Finished Measurements

Finished Chest: 18 [20, 21, 23½] inches

Length: 9 [10, 11, 12] inches

Materials

- Universal Yarn Uptown DK Colors light (DK) weight acrylic yarn (3½ oz/273 yds/100g per ball):
    2 [2, 2, 3] balls #70320 sapphire road *(boy)*
- Universal Yarn Uptown DK light (DK) weight acrylic yarn (3½ oz/273 yds/100g per ball):
    2 [2, 2, 3] balls #156 turquoise *(girl)*
- Size H/8/5mm crochet hook or size needed to obtain gauge
- ½-inch buttons: 4 [4, 4, 5]
- Scrap amounts of black and pink yarn *(girl version only)*
- Tapestry needle
- 2 stitch markers

Gauge

In sc/dc texture pattern: 16 sts and 12 rows = 4 inches

Take time to check gauge.

Pattern Notes

Cardigan is worked in 1 piece from the top down.

Weave in loose ends as work progresses.

Chain-1 at beginning of rows does not count as a stitch.

Chain-3 at beginning of rows counts as first double crochet unless otherwise stated.

Join with slip stitch as indicated unless otherwise stated.

Cardi

Row 1 (WS): Loosely ch 37 [41, 45, 45], sc in 2nd ch from hook and in each ch across, turn. *(36 [40, 44, 44] sc)*

Row 2 (RS): Ch 1 *(see Pattern Notes)*, sc in each of first 4 [0, 4, 2] sc, (2 sc in next sc, sc in each of next 3 [9, 9, 6] sc) 8 [4, 4, 6] times, turn. *(44 [44, 48, 50] sc)*

Row 3: Ch 3 *(see Pattern Notes)*, dc in each of next 5 [5, 6, 7] sc, (2 dc, ch 2, 2 dc) in next sc, dc in each of next 8 sc, (2 dc, ch 2, 2 dc) in next sc, dc in each of next 12 [12, 14, 14] sc, (2 dc, ch 2, 2 dc) in next sc, dc in each of next 8 sc, (2 dc, ch 2, 2 dc) in next sc, dc in each of rem 6 [6, 7, 8] sc, turn. *(56 [56, 60, 62] dc, 4 ch-2 sps)*

Row 4: Ch 1, (sc in each dc across to next ch-2 sp, ch 2, sk next ch-2 sp) 4 times, sc in each rem dc across, ending with sc in top of ch-3 at beg of previous row, turn.

Row 5: Ch 3, (dc in each sc across to next ch-2 sp, {2 dc, ch 2, 2 dc} around both ch-2 sps below) 4 times, dc in each rem sc across, turn. *(72 [72, 76, 78] dc, 4 ch-2 sps)*

Rows 6–11 [6–13, 6–13, 6–15]: Rep (rows 4 and 5) 3 [4, 4, 5] times, turn. *(120 [136, 140, 158] dc, 4 ch-2 sps)*

Last row (RS): Ch 1, sc in each of first 16 [18, 19, 22] dc *(for left front)*, ch 4, sk next 28 [32, 32, 36] dc *(for sleeve)*, sc in each of next 32 [36, 38, 42] dc *(for back)*, ch 4, sk next 28 [32, 32, 36] dc *(for sleeve)*, sc in each of last 16 [18, 19, 22] dc *(for right front)*, turn. *(64 [72, 76, 86] dc, 2 ch-4 sps)*

Body

Row 1 (WS): Ch 3, dc in each sc and in each ch across row, turn. *(72 [80, 84, 94] dc)*

Row 2: Ch 1, sc in each dc across, placing a marker in 18th [21st, 21st, 25th] st from each front edge, ending with sc in top of ch-3 at beg of previous row, turn.

Row 3: Ch 3, dc in each sc across to sc with first marker, 2 dc in marked sc, moving marker to last of these 2 dc made, dc in each sc across to sc with 2nd marker, 2 dc in marked sc, moving marker to first of these 2 dc made, dc in each sc across, turn. *(74 [82, 86, 96] dc)*

Row 4: Ch 1, sc in each dc across, moving the markers to the new sts as you come to them, ending with sc in top of ch-3 at beg of previous row, turn.

Row 5: Ch 3, dc in each sc across, moving the markers to the new sts as you come to them, turn.

Row 6: Rep row 4.

Rows 7–14: (Rep rows 3–6) twice. *(78 [86, 90, 100] sc at end of last row)*

Work even in established pattern until piece measures 9 [10, 11, 12] inches from shoulder, ending with a sc row on RS.

Edging

Rnd 1 (RS): Rotate piece to work up right front edge, ch 1, work approximately 36 [40, 44, 48] sc evenly along front edge, sc in each of the 36 [40, 44, 44] beg chs around neck, work approximately 36 [40, 44, 48] sc evenly down left front edge, sc in each of the 78 [86, 90, 100] sc along bottom edge, **join** *(see Pattern Notes)* in first sc. *(186 [206, 222, 240] sc)*

Girl Version Only

Rnd 2: Ch 1, working from left to right, **reverse sc** *(see Stitch Guide)* in each sc around, join in first reverse sc. Fasten off.

Boy Version Only

Rnds 2 & 3: Ch 1, sc in each sc around, working a ch in each corner at top and bottom of each front edge, join in first sc.

Fasten off.

Sleeves

Row 1 (RS): Join in 3rd ch *(of the 4 chs)* at base of either underarm, ch 1, sc in same ch, sc in next ch, 2 sc around ch-sp in raglan line, sc in each of next 28 [32, 32, 36] dc, 2 sc around ch-sp in raglan line, sc in each of last 2 chs, turn. *(36 [40, 40, 44] sc)*

Row 2: Ch 3, dc in each sc across, turn.

Row 3: Ch 1, **sc dec** *(see Stitch Guide)* in first 2 dc, sc in each dc across to last 2 dc, sc dec in last 2 dc, turn. *(34 [38, 38, 42] dc)*

(Rep rows 2 and 3) 5 [6, 6, 7] times. *(24 [26, 26, 28] sts at end of last row)*

Girl Version Only

Work even in established pattern until sleeve measures approximately 6 [6½, 7½, 8½] inches from armhole, ending with a sc row. Do not turn.

Last row: Ch 1, working from left to right, reverse sc in each sc. Fasten off.

Work the other sleeve in the same way.

Boy Version Only

Work even in established pattern until sleeve measures approximately 5¾ [6¼, 7¼, 8¼] inches from armhole, ending with a sc row. Turn.

Next row (WS): Ch 1, sc in each sc across, turn.

Rep last row.

Fasten off.

Work the other sleeve in the same way.

Assembly
Sew sleeve seams.

Finishing
Sew buttons along right front edge *(boy)* or left front edge *(girl)*.

Sew first button ½ inch below neckline and rem buttons approximately 2 inches apart.

Use sps between sts on opposite front edge as buttonholes.

Weave in ends.

Cat Pockets (Girl Version Only)

Face Circle
Make 2.

Ch 4, join in first ch to form a ring.

Rnd 1: Ch 1, 6 sc in ring, join in first sc. *(6 sc)*

Rnd 2: Ch 1, 2 sc in first sc and in each of the next 5 sc, join in first sc. *(12 sc)*

Rnd 3: Ch 1, sc in first sc, 2 sc in next sc, [sc in next sc, 2 sc in next sc] 5 times, join in first sc. *(18 sc)*

Rnd 4: Ch 1, 2 sc in first sc, sc in each of next 2 sc, [2 sc in next sc, sc in each of next 2 sc] 5 times, join in first sc. *(24 sc)*

Rnd 5: Ch 1, sc in each of first 3 sc, 2 sc in next sc, [sc in each of next 3 sc, 2 sc in next sc] 5 times, join in first sc. *(30 sc)*

Rnd 6: Ch 1, sc in first sc, 2 sc in next sc, sc in each of next 3 sc, [sc in next sc, 2 sc in next sc, sc in each of next 3 sc] 5 times, join in first sc. *(36 sc)*

Sizes 9–12 Months & 18–24 Months Only

Rnd 7: Ch 1, sc in each of first 5 sc, 2 sc in next sc, [sc in each of next 5 sc, 2 sc in next sc] 5 times, join in first sc. *(42 sc)*

Ears

Row 1 (RS): Ch 1, sc in each of first 5 sc, turn, leaving rem sts unworked. *(5 sc)*

Row 2: Ch 1, sc dec in first 2 sc, sc in next sc, sc dec in last 2 sc, turn. *(3 sc)*

Row 3: Ch 1, sc dec in 3 sc at top of ear, work 3 sc evenly along the side of ear *(in row edges)*, sl st in each of next 5 sc on last rnd of face circle, sc in each of next 5 sc, turn.

Row 4: Ch 1, sc dec in first 2 sc, sc in next sc, sc dec in next 2 sc, turn, leaving rem sts unworked. *(3 sc)*

Row 5: Ch 1, sc dec in 3 sc at top of ear, work 3 sc evenly along the side of ear *(in row edges)*, sl st in next sc on last rnd of face circle. Fasten off, leaving a 10-inch-long tail for sewing the pocket to cardi.

Embroider

Using scrap yarn, embroider eyes, nose and whiskers on the face circle *(see picture for colors and placements)*. For the eyes, use **French knots** *(see illustration)* and use **straight stitches** *(see illustration)* for the whiskers and nose.

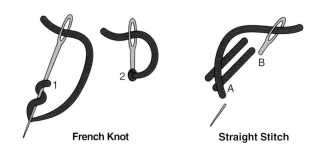

French Knot   Straight Stitch

Finishing

Sew pockets to each front piece, sewing through both fabrics along the bottom edge of face circle from ear to ear.

Weave in ends. ●

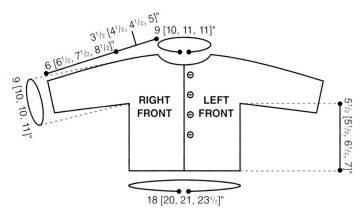

Note: Placement of buttons is reversed for girl version.

Mosaic Shawl

Design by Lena Skvagerson for Annie's Signature Designs

Skill Level

 INTERMEDIATE

Finished Measurements

13 inches wide x 75 inches long

Materials

- Scheepjes Whirl super fine (fingering) weight cotton/acrylic yarn (7½ oz/1,093 yds/215g per cake):
    1 cake #766 mid morning mocha'roo
- Size I/9/5.5mm crochet hook or size needed to obtain gauge
- Tapestry needle

Gauge

13 sts = 4 inches; 24 rows = 4 inches

Take time to check gauge.

Pattern Notes

The pattern is worked with 1 strand from inside of cake (A) and 1 strand from outside of cake (B).

Each row of the chart represents 2 rows worked in same color.

Each row of the chart is first read from right to left (right side, odd rows), and then from left to right (wrong side, even rows).

Each color is used for 2 rows; the color on your hook when you turn at the end of a row is the color you will use for the next row.

For all rows worked with color A, an empty square on the chart represents a chain-2 and a square with an X represents a single crochet. It is the opposite for all rows worked with color B (empty = single crochet, X = chain-2).

When working on the right side with A, each square with an X directly over another square with an X means there will be a **dc in next sk st** (see Special Stitch).

When working on the right side with B, each empty square over another empty square means there will be a dc in next sk st.

Special Stitch

Double crochet in next skipped stitch (dc in next sk st): Working in front of ch-2 sp, dc in next sk st 3 rows below.

Shawl

Row 1 (RS): With **color A** (see Pattern Notes), ch 44, sc in 2nd ch from hook and in each ch across, turn. (43 sc)

Row 2 (WS): Ch 1, sc in each sc across, **changing to color B** (see illustration) in last sc, turn.

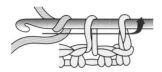

Single Crochet Color Change

Row 3: Ch 1, sc in first sc, [sc in each of next 2 sc, ch 2, sk next sc, sc in each of next 5 sc, ch 2, sk next sc, sc in next sc] 4 times, sc in each of last 2 sc, turn.

Row 4: Ch 1, sc in each of first 2 sc, [sc in next sc, ch 2, sk next sp, sc in each of next 5 sc, ch 2, sk next sp, sc in each of next 2 sc] 4 times, sc in last sc, changing to color A, turn.

Row 5: Ch 1, sc in first sc, [sc in next sc, ch 2, sk next sc, **dc in next sk st** (see Special Stitch and Pattern Notes), sc in each of next 2 sc, ch 2, sk next sc, sc in each of next 2 sc, dc in next sk st, ch 2, sk next st] 4 times, sc in each of last 2 sc, turn.

Row 6: Ch 1, sc in each of first 2 sc, [(ch 2, sk next sp, sc in each of next 3 sts) twice, ch 2, sk next sp, sc in next sc] 4 times, sc in last sc, changing to color B, turn.

Row 7: Ch 1, sc in first sc, [ch 2, sk next sc, dc in next sk st, sc in each of next 2 sc, ch 2, sk next sc, dc in next sk st, ch 2, sk next st, sc in each of next 2 sc, dc in next sk st] across, ch 2, sk next sc, sc in last sc, turn.

Row 8: Ch 1, sc in first sc, ch 2, sk next sp, [sc in each of next 3 sts, ch 2, sk next sp, sc in next st, ch 2, sk next sp, sc in each of next 3 sts, ch 2, sk next sp] 4 times, sc in last sc, changing to color A, turn.

Row 9: Ch 1, sc in first sc, [dc in next sk st, sc in each of next 2 sc, ch 2, sk next sc, dc in next sk st, sc in next sc, dc in next sk st, ch 2, sk next st, sc in each of next 2 sc] 4 times, dc in next sk st, sc in last sc, turn.

Row 10: Ch 1, sc in each of first 2 sts, [sc in each of next 2 sc, ch 2, sk next sp, sc in each of next 3 sts, ch 2, sk next sp, sc in each of next 3 sts] 4 times, sc in last sc, changing to color B, turn.

Row 11: Ch 1, sc in first sc, [sc in each of next 2 sc, ch 2, sk next sc, dc in next sk st, sc in each of next 3 sc, dc in next sk st, ch 2, sk next sc, sc in next sc] 4 times, sc in each of last 2 sc, turn.

Rep [Rows 4–11] for pattern until you reach section of cake where A and B are no longer contrasting, ending with any WS row.

Fasten off. ●

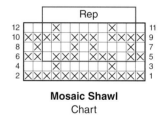

Mosaic Shawl
Chart

KEY
☒ Sc when using A, ch-2 when using B
☐ Sc when using B, ch-2 when using A

Faux-Macramé Plant Hanger

Design by Laurie Ann Sand

Skill Level

 ◼◼☐☐ **EASY**

Finished Measurements

Fits pot with flat bottom and sloping sides that is 5½ inches tall, 3 inches in diameter at the bottom and 7 inches in diameter at the top.

Materials

- Lily Sugar'n Cream Super Size medium (worsted) weight cotton yarn (4 oz/200 yds/113g per ball): 1 ball #818004 ecru
- Size F/5/3.75mm crochet hook or size needed to obtain gauge
- 6 x 3-inch piece stiff cardboard or tassel maker
- Tapestry needle

4 MEDIUM

Gauge

First 3 rnds of pattern = 3 inches in diameter

Gauge is important for this project as the hanger should fit very tightly over the pot. Take time to check gauge.

Pattern Notes

Weave in loose ends as work progresses.

Join with slip stitch as indicated unless otherwise stated.

Pattern is worked in the round without turning throughout, with where to join described in the pattern instructions for each round. The location of the join will sometimes change to maintain the appearance of the pattern.

Special Stitches

Picot: Ch 3, sl st in 3rd ch from hook (see illustration).

Hanging cord: Ch 101, sc in 2nd ch from hook and in each rem ch across.

Picot

Plant Hanger

Rnd 1: Form a **slip ring** (see illustration), or ch 4 and **join** (see Pattern Notes) to 4th ch from hook to form a ring. Ch 1, 9 sc into ring, tighten slip ring, join to first sc. (9 sc)

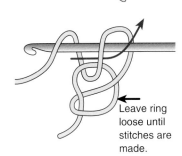

4" end

Leave ring loose until stitches are made.

Slip Ring

Rnd 2: Ch 1, 2 sc in first sc, 2 sc in each rem sc around, join to first sc. (18 sc)

Rnd 3: Ch 1, sc in first sc, *picot (see Special Stitches), sc in each of next 2 sc; rep from * 7 times, picot, sc in last sc, join to first sc. (18 sc, 9 picots)

Rnd 4: Ch 1, sc in first sc, *ch 6, sk picot, sc in each of next 2 sc; rep from * 7 times, ch 6, sk picot, sc in last sc, join to first sc. (18 sc, 9 ch-6 sps)

Rnd 5: Ch 1, sc in first sc, *6 sc in next ch-6 sp, sc in next sc, picot, sc in next sc; rep from * 7 times, 6 sc in last ch-6 sp, sc in last sc, picot, join to first sc. (72 sc, 9 picots)

Rnd 6: Sl st in next 4 sc (start of rnd has moved), ch 1, sc in same st as last sl st, *ch 6, sk next (3 sc, picot, 3 sc), sc in each of next 2 sc; rep from * 7 times, ch 6, sk next (3 sc, picot, 3 sc), sc in last sc (work over sl st), join to first sc. (18 sc, 9 ch-6 sps)

Rnds 7–13: Rep [rnds 5 and 6] 3 times, then rep rnd 5 once more.

Rnd 14: Sl st in next 4 sc (start of rnd has moved), ch 1, sc in same st as last sl st, *ch 4, sk next (3 sc, picot, 3 sc), sc in each of next 2 sc; rep from * 7 times, ch 4, sk next (3 sc, picot, 3 sc), sc in last sc (work over sl st), join to first sc. (18 sc, 9 ch-4 sps)

Rnd 15: Ch 1, sc in first st, *4 sc in next ch-4 sp, sc in each of next 2 sc; rep from * 7 times, 4 sc in last ch-4 sp, sc in last sc, join to first sc. (54 sc)

Rnd 16: Ch 1, sc in first st, sc in each of next 6 sc, work **hanging cord** (see Special Stitches), sc in next 14 sc, work hanging cord, sc in next 13 sc, work hanging cord, sc in next 14 sc, work hanging cord, sc in each of last 6 sc, join to first sc. Fasten off. (54 sc, 4 hanging cords)

Tassel

Ch 30 and fasten off.

Wrap yarn around length of cardboard 45 times. Thread the yarn ch under the wraps and tie ends of ch tog with an overhand knot (see illustration A). Slide the ch so the knotted end is under the wraps. Gently remove the wraps from cardboard. Tie the end of the working yarn around the wraps about an inch beneath the ch (see illustration B), continue to wrap the yarn around the wraps several times. Cut yarn and tuck the end under itself to secure. Cut the bottom lps of the tassel. Hang the tassel from the center/bottom of the plant hanger using the yarn ch.

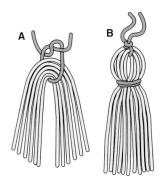

A B

Tassel

Finishing

Block as follows: Soak in lukewarm water, squeeze out excess moisture, stretch the hanger over the bottom of the pot, and allow to dry completely with pot upside down.

When dry, tie the hanging cords tog at the desired length with an overhand knot. ●

STITCH GUIDE

Need help? ▶ **StitchGuide.com** • ILLUSTRATED GUIDES • HOW-TO VIDEOS

STITCH ABBREVIATIONS

beg	begin/begins/beginning
bpdc	back post double crochet
bpsc	back post single crochet
bptr	back post treble crochet
CC	contrasting color
ch(s)	chain(s)
ch-	refers to chain or space previously made (i.e., ch-1 space)
ch sp(s)	chain space(s)
cl(s)	cluster(s)
cm	centimeter(s)
dc	double crochet (singular/plural)
dc dec	double crochet 2 or more stitches together, as indicated
dec	decrease/decreases/decreasing
dtr	double treble crochet
ext	extended
fpdc	front post double crochet
fpsc	front post single crochet
fptr	front post treble crochet
g	gram(s)
hdc	half double crochet
hdc dec	half double crochet 2 or more stitches together, as indicated
inc	increase/increases/increasing
lp(s)	loop(s)
MC	main color
mm	millimeter(s)
oz	ounce(s)
pc	popcorn(s)
rem	remain/remains/remaining
rep(s)	repeat(s)
rnd(s)	round(s)
RS	right side
sc	single crochet (singular/plural)
sc dec	single crochet 2 or more stitches together, as indicated
sk	skip/skipped/skipping
sl st(s)	slip stitch(es)
sp(s)	space(s)/spaced
st(s)	stitch(es)
tog	together
tr	treble crochet
trtr	triple treble
WS	wrong side
yd(s)	yard(s)
yo	yarn over

YARN CONVERSION

OUNCES TO GRAMS	GRAMS TO OUNCES
1 .... 28.4	25 .... ⅞
2 .... 56.7	40 .... 1⅔
3 .... 85.0	50 .... 1¾
4 .... 113.4	100 .... 3½

UNITED STATES		UNITED KINGDOM
sl st (slip stitch)	=	sc (single crochet)
sc (single crochet)	=	dc (double crochet)
hdc (half double crochet)	=	htr (half treble crochet)
dc (double crochet)	=	tr (treble crochet)
tr (treble crochet)	=	dtr (double treble crochet)
dtr (double treble crochet)	=	ttr (triple treble crochet)
skip	=	miss

Reverse single crochet (reverse sc): Ch 1, sk first st, working from left to right, insert hook in next st from front to back, draw up lp on hook, yo and draw through both lps on hook.

Chain (ch): Yo, pull through lp on hook.

Single crochet (sc): Insert hook in st, yo, pull through st, yo, pull through both lps on hook.

Double crochet (dc): Yo, insert hook in st, yo, pull through st, [yo, pull through 2 lps] twice.

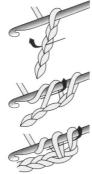

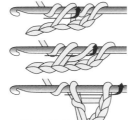

Front loop (front lp) Back loop (back lp)

Front Loop   Back Loop

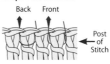

Front post stitch (fp): Back post stitch (bp): When working post st, insert hook from right to left around post of st on previous row.

Back   Front

Post of Stitch

Half double crochet (hdc): Yo, insert hook in st, yo, pull through st, yo, pull through all 3 lps on hook.

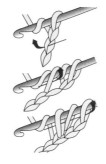

Double treble crochet (dtr): Yo 3 times, insert hook in st, yo, pull through st, [yo, pull through 2 lps] 4 times.

Slip stitch (sl st): Insert hook in st, pull through both lps on hook.

Chain color change (ch color change) Yo with new color, draw through last lp on hook.

Double crochet color change (dc color change) Drop first color, yo with new color, draw through last 2 lps of st.

Treble crochet (tr): Yo twice, insert hook in st, yo, pull through st, [yo, pull through 2 lps] 3 times.

Single crochet decrease (sc dec): (Insert hook, yo, draw lp through) in each of the sts indicated, yo, draw through all lps on hook.

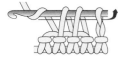

Example of 2-sc dec

Half double crochet decrease (hdc dec): (Yo, insert hook, yo, draw lp through) in each of the sts indicated, yo, draw through all lps on hook.

Example of 2-hdc dec

Double crochet decrease (dc dec): (Yo, insert hook, yo, draw lp through, yo, draw through 2 lps on hook) in each of the sts indicated, yo, draw through all lps on hook.

Example of 2-dc dec

Treble crochet decrease (tr dec): Holding back last lp of each st, tr in each of the sts indicated, yo, pull through all lps on hook.

Example of 2-tr dec

Metric Conversion Charts

METRIC CONVERSIONS

yards	x	.9144	=	meters (m)
yards	x	91.44	=	centimeters (cm)
inches	x	2.54	=	centimeters (cm)
inches	x	25.40	=	millimeters (mm)
inches	x	.0254	=	meters (m)

centimeters	x	.3937	=	inches
meters	x	1.0936	=	yards

INCHES INTO MILLIMETERS & CENTIMETERS (Rounded off slightly)

inches	mm	cm	inches	cm	inches	cm	inches	cm
1/8	3	0.3	5	12.5	21	53.5	38	96.5
1/4	6	0.6	5 1/2	14	22	56	39	99
3/8	10	1	6	15	23	58.5	40	101.5
1/2	13	1.3	7	18	24	61	41	104
5/8	15	1.5	8	20.5	25	63.5	42	106.5
3/4	20	2	9	23	26	66	43	109
7/8	22	2.2	10	25.5	27	68.5	44	112
1	25	2.5	11	28	28	71	45	114.5
1 1/4	32	3.2	12	30.5	29	73.5	46	117
1 1/2	38	3.8	13	33	30	76	47	119.5
1 3/4	45	4.5	14	35.5	31	79	48	122
2	50	5	15	38	32	81.5	49	124.5
2 1/2	65	6.5	16	40.5	33	84	50	127
3	75	7.5	17	43	34	86.5		
3 1/2	90	9	18	46	35	89		
4	100	10	19	48.5	36	91.5		
4 1/2	115	11.5	20	51	37	94		

KNITTING NEEDLES CONVERSION CHART

Canada/U.S.	0	1	2	3	4	5	6	7	8	9	10	10½	11	13	15
Metric (mm)	2	2¼	2¾	3¼	3½	3¾	4	4½	5	5½	6	6½	8	9	10

CROCHET HOOKS CONVERSION CHART

Canada/U.S.	1/B	2/C	3/D	4/E	5/F	6/G	7	8/H	9/I	10/J	10½/K	N
Metric (mm)	2.25	2.75	3.25	3.5	3.75	4	4.5	5	5.5	6	6.5	9.0

Annie's® Published by Annie's, 306 East Parr Road, Berne, IN 46711. Printed in USA. Copyright © 2022 Annie's. All rights reserved. This publication may not be reproduced in part or in whole without written permission from the publisher.

RETAIL STORES: If you would like to carry this publication or any other Annie's publication, visit AnniesWSL.com.

Every effort has been made to ensure that the instructions in this publication are complete and accurate. We cannot, however, take responsibility for human error, typographical mistakes or variations in individual work. Please visit AnniesCustomerService.com to check for pattern updates.

ISBN: 978-1-64025-559-3

1 2 3 4 5 6 7 8 9